Mass, Sa

THE CATHOLIC FAITH SERIES

Volume Two

Libreria Editrice Vaticana

United States Conference of Catholic Bishops
Washington, DC

English translation copyright © 2012, Libreria Editrice Vaticana. All rights reserved.

Excerpts from the English translation of *The Roman Missal* © 2010 International Commission on English in the Liturgy Corportation. All rights reserved.

Scripture excerpts used in this work are taken from the *New American Bible, revised edition* © 2010, 1991, 1986, 1970 Confraternity of Christian Doctrine, Inc., Washington, DC. All rights reserved. No part of this work may be reproduced or transmitted in any form or by any means, electronic or mechanical, including photocopying, recording, or by any information storage and retrieval system, without permission in writing from the copyright owner.

Excerpts from the *Catechism of the Catholic Church*, second edition, copyright © 2000, Libreria Editrice Vaticana–United States Conference of Catholic Bishops, Washington, DC. Used with permission. All rights reserved.

Quotations from *Code of Canon Law: Latin-English Edition: New English Translation* (*Codex Iuris Canonici* [CIC]) copyright © 1998, Canon Law Society of America, Washington, DC. Used with permission. All rights reserved.

Excerpts from *The Documents of Vatican II*, Walter M. Abbott, SJ, General Editor, copyright © 1966 by America Press, Inc. Reprinted with permission. All rights reserved.

Illustration: "Secret of the Meal" by Sister Marie-Paul Faran, OSB. Used with permission from The Printery House. All rights reserved.

ISBN 978-1-60137-338-0

First printing, December 2012

Contents

Preface v

I. Holy Mass: Why Go Every Sunday? 1

II. Sunday 15

III. Sacred Images 27

IV. Liturgical Vesture 40

V. Why Baptize Babies? 53

VI. When and How to Confess 73

VII. Forming Conscience 84

VIII. What Is Moral Conscience? 96

IX. Priesthood 114

X. Clerical Celibacy	123
XI. How to Pray	136
XII. How Christians Meditate	148
XIII. Lent	163
XIV. Mary	171
XV. The Rosary	189
XVI. Indulgences	202

Preface

How did the project for this book come about?

For about three years, I have been placing in the Basilica of San Carlo al Corso (Rome), of which I am rector, some catechetical pamphlets on topics related to current events, available to anyone who comes into the basilica. And to my surprise I noticed that more than 2.5 million pamphlets have been taken by people passing through the basilica. So in response to the demand from so many people, I decided to collect, in a compact and portable format, the pamphlets in question.

What criterion was used to select the topics?

The criterion of relevance. I decided to present brief summaries of what the Catholic Church teaches about some of the timely topics that are being brought to people's attention now for various reasons. In some cases I have also tried to select topics that are somewhat forgotten by many Christians today, or even disputed by some of them.

What documents were used in addressing these topics?

Mainly the documents of the Holy See, and for two reasons. First, because these documents tend to be overlooked by the general public, and their richness, comprehensiveness, and beauty deserve to be more widely known. Second, because they express essential and fundamental beliefs that are held not by any one Catholic alone, but by the Catholic Church as a whole, transmitted through the Magisterium of the pope and the bishops. This Magisterium was established by Christ himself, to confirm the faith of individual believers in him so that down through the centuries and in various parts of the world all may profess one and the same Catholic faith.

Why are the topics presented in dialogue form?

From an editorial point of view, the topics are presented in the form of a dialogue, with questions followed by briefly summarized answers.

This dialogue form tends to be more inviting for the reader, and also continues a constant and long-standing catechetical tradition in the history of the Church. Many catechisms that have formed entire generations have used, and very fruitfully, this didactical system of question and answer.

It must also not be forgotten that the Christian faith itself, a special gift from God, is a continual dialogue of God with man, and of man with God.

I also think that it corresponds to the needs of the contemporary world, in which journalistic-style interviews are preferred, as well as summarized formulations, partly because of the little time that many people, even those who identify themselves as Catholic, now set aside for the catechetical study of their own faith. And this lack of time unfortunately leads to religious ignorance, which in turn leads to widespread relativism, to an arbitrary subjectivism, and last but not least to a distressing vacuum of knowledge about the contents of the faith, which characterizes not only children and young people in their catechetical journey but also adults in their varied and demanding activities.

What is the purpose of this book?

It may help people to understand better the beauty and the importance of the response that the Christian faith offers to all on some topics that characterize our society even today.

This book contains only some of the elements that make up the rich and mysterious panorama of the Catholic faith, and only some of the problems that are eating away at the world today. At the same time, I want to emphasize that in dealing with the individual topics, I do not intend to present all of their aspects and elements, and therefore I do not mean to give each argument exhaustive and complete treatment, but to offer only a few thoughts, fragments of reflection.

So it is intended both for Christians, whom it may provide with an opportunity for a better and deeper understanding of the elements of their faith, and for anyone who might wish to know what the Catholic Church, through some of its official documents, believes and lives, with the help of God.

> His Excellency Raffaello Martinelli
> Bishop of Frascati
> Frascati, September 12, 2010
> First anniversary of my episcopal ordination

I
Holy Mass: Why Go Every Sunday?

What is the Holy Mass?

✠ The Holy Mass is

- The celebration of the Paschal Mystery-Sacrifice (Passion, Death, Resurrection) of Christ the Lord, made present and effective within the Christian community: "We proclaim your Death, O Lord, and profess your Resurrection until you come again."
- The true, real, substantial presence of Christ with his Body, Blood, soul, and divinity: true God and true Man
- The banquet-communion with Christ, and, through him, with our brothers and sisters. Through his

sacrifice, Christ unites us in a wonderful manner to himself and among ourselves, "so that they may be one" (Jn 17:22).

✠ In the Holy Mass, Christ

- Gives praise and thanks to God the Father (Eucharist)
- Actualizes his Paschal Sacrifice (memorial)
- Makes himself really present with his Body and Blood in the bread and wine consecrated in the power of the Holy Spirit (transubstantiation)
- Makes himself our food and drink for our eternal salvation (banquet)
- Realizes the new and eternal covenant between God and humanity in the sacrifice of his own Body and Blood, not with the blood of animals (see Old Testament)

Who instituted the Holy Mass?

Christ the Lord instituted the Holy Mass on Holy Thursday, the night on which he was betrayed. In this way he anticipated and accepted the sacrifice of himself that he would offer the next day on the Cross.

What does it mean that the Holy Mass is the memorial of the sacrifice of Christ?

The Holy Mass is a memorial in the sense that it makes present and efficacious upon the altar, in an unbloody manner, that sacrifice that Christ, in a bloody manner, offered to the Father on Calvary for the salvation of all people.

The Holy Mass is not, therefore, only the memory of past events but makes present and actual the one perfect sacrifice of Christ on the Cross. The priest and the victim are the same: Christ. The purpose is the same: the salvation of all. It is the manner of the offering that is different: bloody on the cross of Calvary, unbloody in the Holy Mass.

What does transubstantiation mean?

It means that in the Holy Mass, through the power of the Holy Spirit, the bread and wine become, in their substance, the Body and Blood of Christ.

✠ The doctrine of transubstantiation is a truth of faith that is already evident in Sacred Scripture and was afterward confirmed by the Fathers of the Church. "The Catholic Church has always displayed and still displays this latria that ought to be paid to the Sacrament of the Eucharist" (Pope Paul VI, *Mysterium Fidei*, no. 56).

✠ "That the true Body and the true Blood of Christ is present in this sacrament cannot be learned through the senses, but only through faith, which is based upon the authority of God" (St. Thomas Aquinas, *Summa Theologiae*, III, 75, 1).

What is the relationship between the Holy Mass and the Church?

✠ The Eucharist expresses and builds the Church, as authentic communion of the People of God, in its rich plurality and in its intimate unity. The Eucharistic bread itself, made up of many grains, and the wine, made of many grapes, signify the unity and plurality of the Christian people that celebrates the Eucharist.

✠ The Eucharist makes the Church, in the sense that the Eucharist gathers it, manifests it, nourishes it, strengthens it, makes it grow in quality and sends it out to all humanity.

✠ And at the same time, the Church makes the Eucharist, it celebrates it, offers it to the Father together with Christ and the Holy Spirit.

✠ The Church finds in the Eucharist its icon, its model. The Church, in its daily life, must make itself Eucharist: sacrifice (an offering that dies and rises, pleasing to the Father), presence, communion. The Church therefore does not only celebrate and adore, but also imitates the Eucharist.

✠ The Eucharist is the summit of the liturgy. It is the compendium and the summary of our faith. It contains the whole spiritual treasury of the Church, which is Christ himself, our Passover and our living bread. It is the privileged place in which the Church confesses its faith and confesses it in the highest and most complete way possible.

How does the Holy Mass involve daily life?

✠ The Holy Mass constitutes the center, the heart of all Christian life for the ecclesial community, universal and local, and for the individual faithful.

In fact, the Holy Mass

- Is the culmination of the action with which God sanctifies the world in Christ, and of the worship that human beings give to the Father
- Is the source and summit of all Christian life. It puts itself at the center of ecclesial life. It unites heaven and earth. It embraces and pervades all of creation.
- Is the point of arrival and departure for every activity of the Christian community and of every believer. It is from the Holy Mass that one goes out to the world, to one's daily activities with the commitment to live out that which has been celebrated (Mass—mandate—mission in the world).

  It is to the Holy Mass that one returns with all the rich experience of work (Eucharist, offering and praise for everything that one has done through Christ).
- Is the center, the norm, the model, and the most sublime moment of every prayer of the Church and of the individual Christian
- Is the appointment of love, weekly or even daily, with the One who has given all of himself for us
- Is the Sacrament that manifests and actualizes the mystery of Christ, the very mystery of the human person, which expresses and realizes itself fully in the Holy Mass

✠ The Holy Mass is food, light, and strength for our earthly pilgrimage and arouses and fosters our desire for eternal life: heaven.

Is there a prayer that is equal or superior to the Holy Mass?

Absolutely not. The Holy Mass exceeds the scope of other prayers, and in fact no other action of the Church matches its efficacy in nature and degree. It is the most valuable thing that the Church could have on its journey through history. In it is contained all the spiritual good of the Church.

Is it obligatory to participate in the Holy Mass?

Christians have an obligation to participate in the Holy Mass every Sunday and on holy days of obligation unless there are serious circumstances (illness, etc.). Without a serious reason, the Christian who does not fulfill this obligation commits a mortal sin.

The Sunday Eucharist is "a matter of identity," or better, it is a vital necessity that cannot be ignored.

Why is it obligatory on Sunday in particular?

Because Jesus Christ rose "on the first day of the week" (Lk 24:1), the *dies solis* (day of the sun), later called *dies Domini:* Sunday (see St. Justin, *First Apology*, ch. 65/67). And the Resurrection of Christ is the central event of the entire life of Christ and of our Christian faith. "If Christ has not been raised, then empty [too] is our preaching; empty, too, your faith" (1 Cor 15:14).

How is Sunday made holy?

✠ By participating in the Holy Mass

✠ By dedicating ourselves to those activities that permit us to

- Render worship to God (more time dedicated to personal and family prayer, to faith-building reading and study groups, to cemetery visits . . .)
- Take care of our marital and family life
- Ensure the proper and necessary rest of body and spirit
- Dedicate ourselves to works of charity, above all in service of the sick, the elderly, the poor . . .

What must our attitude be toward the Holy Mass?

The Holy Mass, because of what it is, requires from us

- A great faith ("mystery of faith") that allows us to embrace all the richness of the mystery
- Constant willingness to explore, through catechesis, what is celebrated, so that it may become Life in our lives
- Adequate formation in view of a full, conscious, and active participation in the Eucharistic celebration
- Joyful and communal participation. Precisely because the Holy Mass has a communitarian character, great importance is taken on by
  - The dialogue between the celebrant and the assembly

- The singing, a sign of heartfelt joy: "Those who sing well pray twice."
- The gestures and postures (standing, kneeling, sitting, etc.) that express and foster the intention and the interior sentiments of participation, and that are a sign of the unity of spirit of all the participants

- Purity of conscience. Only those who are at peace with God and with their brothers and sisters participate fully and efficaciously in the Holy Mass.
- Complete participation. This involves
  - Punctuality in arriving at church for the beginning of the Holy Mass
  - Attentive participation in the banquet of the Word of God
  - Sharing in the banquet of the Body of Christ ("Take this, all of you, and eat of it . . .")

When participating in the Holy Mass, is it necessary to receive Holy Communion?

It is very good for Catholics, every time they participate in the Holy Mass, to receive Holy Communion as well. But it should not be received more than twice a day.

Who can receive Holy Communion?

Holy Communion can be received by any Catholic who is in the grace of God, which means that, after carefully examining his or her conscience, he or she is not aware of being in a state of mortal sin, because in that case he or she would commit a sacrilege: "Therefore whoever eats the bread or drinks the cup of the Lord unworthily will have to answer for the body and blood of the Lord . . . For anyone who eats and drinks without discerning the body, eats and drinks judgment on himself" (1 Cor 11:27, 29).

How should one approach Holy Communion?

✠ With respect: the attitude of the body (gestures, dignified clothing) must also express the respect, the solemnity, the joy of this encounter with the Lord.

✠ With fasting for at least one hour

✠ After participating, from the beginning, in the Holy Mass, and making a commitment to thank the Lord for the great gift received, even after the Holy Mass and during the day and week

Why is it important to respect the liturgical norms in the Holy Mass?

✠ The liturgical norms

- Express and protect the Holy Mass, which, as a work of Christ the Priest and of his Body which is the Church, is the sacred action par excellence
- Make it possible to respect and actualize the intrinsic relationship between the profession and celebration of the faith, the *lex orandi* and *lex credendi*. The sacred

liturgy, in fact, is intimately connected to the principles of doctrine, and the use of unapproved texts and rites entails, as a result, the weakening or loss of the necessary connection between the *lex orandi* and the *lex credendi*.

- Are an expression of the authentic ecclesial sense. They are the conduit of the whole faith and tradition of the Church.

   The Holy Mass is never the private property of anyone, neither of the celebrant nor of the community in which the mysteries are celebrated. Obedience to the liturgical norms must be rediscovered and appreciated as a reflection and testimony of the one universal Church, made present in every celebration of the Eucharist.

- Guarantee the validity, the dignity, and the decorum of the liturgical action, and with it also Christ's making himself present
- Lead to the conformity of our sentiments with those of Christ, expressed in the words and rites of the liturgy
- Express and guarantee the "right" of the faithful to a worthy celebration, and therefore also their right to demand it

Whenever violations or abuses are found, the faithful should report them, in truth and with charity, to the legitimate authority (to the bishop or the Holy See).

✠ "No one, then, may take it on himself to make changes, substitutions, deletions, or additions. There is special reason to keep the Order of Mass intact" (*Liturgicae Instaurationes*, 3; see also *Sacrosanctum Concilium*, no. 22 §3).

✠ "Each particular Church must be in accord with the universal Church not only regarding the doctrine of the faith and sacramental signs, but also as to the usages universally received from apostolic and unbroken tradition. These are to be kept not only so that errors may be avoided, but also so that the faith may be handed on in its integrity, since the Church's rule of prayer (*lex orandi*) corresponds to her rule of faith (*lex credendi*)" (*General Instruction of the Roman Missal* [GIRM], no. 397).

What harm is caused by liturgical abuses?

✠ Liturgical abuses not only distort the celebration, but they create uncertainty about doctrine, confusion, and scandal among the people of God. Lack of respect for the liturgical norms contributes to obscuring true Catholic faith and doctrine on this marvelous Sacrament. Liturgical abuses, rather than being an expression of freedom, demonstrate a superficial understanding or even ignorance of the great biblical and ecclesial tradition relative to the Eucharist that is expressed in these norms.

✠ The mystery entrusted to our hands is too great for anyone to presume to treat it according to any personal whim, which would not respect its sacred character and universal dimension.

If there is no Holy Mass (in the absence of a priest), how does one fulfill the Sunday precept?

This is what the Church recommends in this regard:

✠ The faithful can go to one of the churches of the diocese at which the Holy Mass is celebrated, even when this requires a certain sacrifice.

✠ Where long distances make it practically impossible to participate in the Sunday Eucharist, it is important that Christian communities gather nonetheless to praise the Lord and commemorate the day that is dedicated to him.

In this case, it is necessary to keep in mind that

- There is a big difference between the Holy Mass and Sunday assemblies in the absence of a priest.
- The Liturgy of the Word, organized under the guidance of a deacon or leader of the community to whom this ministry has been granted by the competent authority, should be carried out according to a specific ritual designed and approved by the conference of bishops.
- It is up to the local bishop to grant permission to distribute Communion at these liturgies, after carefully evaluating the appropriateness of this decision.
- These assemblies must not

- Create confusion about the central role of the priest and about the sacramental component in the life of the Church
- Give rise to views of the Church that are not in keeping with the truth of the Gospel and of the tradition of the Church
- They can be special occasions to pray that God may send holy priests according to his heart

✠ Priests should make practical and concrete efforts to visit the communities entrusted to their pastoral care as often as possible so that these may not remain for too long without the Eucharistic celebration (see Pope Benedict XVI, postsynodal apostolic exhortation *Sacramentum Caritatis*, no. 75).

What have some of the saints said about the Eucharist?

✠ "If you are the Body of Christ and its members, then your own mystery lies upon the Eucharistic table. You must be what you see, and you must receive what you are" (St. Augustine).

✠ "Only the Church can offer to the Creator this pure oblation (the Eucharist), offering to him with thanksgiving that which comes from his creation" (St. Irenaeus).

✠ "The Word of Christ, which was able to create from nothing that which did not exist, can it not transform into a different substance that which exists?" (St. Ambrose).

✠ "The Eucharist is practically the crowning of the entire spiritual life and the end to which all the sacraments are directed" (St. Thomas).

✠

For more on this topic, see the following pontifical documents:

Paul VI, *Mysterium Fidei*, 1965
John Paul II, *Dominicae Cenae*, 1980, *Ecclesia de Eucaristia*, 2003
Benedict XVI, *Sacramentum Caritatis*, 2007
Catechism of the Catholic Church, nos. 1322-1419
Compendium of the CCC, nos. 271-294
Congregation for Divine Worship and the Sacraments, *Redemptionis Sacramentum*, 2004
Vatican Council II, *Sacrosanctum Concilium*

II
Sunday

Why is Sunday important for the Christian?

Because Christ rose on Sunday. And in fact, it was Sunday when the women who had been present at the Crucifixion of Christ went to the tomb "very early when the sun had risen, on the first day of the week" (Mk 16:2), and found him alive.

Why is the Resurrection of Christ so important?

✠ Because the Resurrection of Jesus is the fundamental, central, and original reality on which the Christian faith is based. "If Christ has not been raised, then empty [too] is our preaching; empty, too, your faith" (1 Cor 15:14).

✠ The Resurrection of Christ is the astonishing event that not only distinguishes itself in an absolutely singular way in human history but is also located at the center of the mystery of time and history. To Christ belong time and the ages. He is the foundation of history, the source of the mystery of the origins and final destination of the world.

What expressions are used to refer to Sunday?

Sunday is also called the day of the Lord, of the Church, of man, of the sun; the first day of the week; the eighth day.

Why is Sunday called

✠ The day of the Lord?

Because Sunday is the day of the celebration of the Passover (Passion, Death, Resurrection, Ascension) of the Lord for the salvation of the world. The Eucharist, which is celebrated on Sunday, is the memorial of this Passover—it makes present and efficacious today the Passover that the Lord accomplished two thousand years ago. This is why Sunday is also referred to as a weekly "Easter." At the same time, the "day of the Lord" is also called the "lord of days," the "primordial feast," in that "all things came to be through him, and without him nothing came to be" (Jn 1:3).

✠ The day of the Church?

Sunday is also called the day of the Church in that, in the Sunday Eucharistic celebration, the Christian community rediscovers its source and summit, the reason for its existence, the origin of its well-being, its true and irreplaceable principle of action. It is around the Sunday Eucharist that the community grows and matures in its mission to communicate the Gospel and to share the intense experience of community among all its members.

✠ The day of man?

As the day of man, Sunday, with its festive dimension, involves the human being in his or her personal, family, and community identity in the logic of a transcendent way of being and living. At the same time, Sunday reveals to the human person the meaning of his or her being and acting.

✠ The first day of the week?

Sunday is also called the first day of the week, because in the Jewish conception, the holy day is Saturday, so Sunday is the first day of the week.

Why is it important to refer to Sunday as "the first day of the week"? Referring to Sunday as the first day of the week emphasizes the singular connection that exists between the Resurrection and creation, between "the first day of the week" on which the Resurrection of Christ took place and the first day of the cosmic week in which God created the world (see Gn 1:1-2, 4). In fact, the Resurrection is tantamount to the beginning of a new creation, of which Christ, "the firstborn of all creation" (Col 1:15), also constitutes the firstfruits, "the firstborn from the dead" (Col 1:18).

✠ The eighth day?

Sunday is also called the eighth day because in the Jewish conception, Saturday is the seventh day of the week, and therefore Sunday is also the eighth day.

What does understanding Sunday as the eighth day emphasize? The eighth day emphasizes the connection between Sunday and eternity. In fact, Sunday, in addition to being the first day, is also the "eighth day," which means that it is situated, with respect to the seven-day cycle, in a unique and transcendent place, which evokes not only the beginning of time, but also its end in the "future age." In this sense, Sunday

- Signifies the truly new and unique day that will follow the current age, the day without end that will know neither evening or morning, the imperishable age that cannot grow old
- Is the incessant preannouncement of the life without end, of the eternal life toward which the Christian is oriented
- Prefigures the last day, that of the Parousia, which is already anticipated in a certain way by the glory of Christ in the event of the Resurrection. In effect, everything that will take place until the end of the world will be nothing but an expansion and manifestation of what took place on the day in which the ravaged Body of the Crucified One was raised.
- Is an invitation to look ahead, it is the day on which the Christian community cries out to Christ its "*Marana tha*—Come, O Lord!" (see 1 Cor 16:22). In this cry of hope and anticipation, it accompanies and supports the hope of humanity.

✠ The day of the sun?

This expression "day of the sun" attributed to Sunday comes from very far away.

At the beginning of the history of Christianity, a perceptive pastoral intuition suggested to the Church to Christianize, for Sunday, the connotation of "day of the sun," an expression that the Romans used for this day and that still appears in some contemporary languages. In this way, the primitive Church protected the faithful from the seductions of cults that divinized the sun and directed the celebration of this day to Christ, the true "sun" of humanity, "the daybreak from on high [that] will visit us to shine on those who sit in darkness and death's shadow" (Lk 1:78-79), come as "a light for revelation to the Gentiles" (Lk 2:32), and who will return at the end of time to transfigure with his dazzling light everyone and everything.

In what sense does Sunday reveal the meaning of time to humanity?

Sunday, flowing from the Resurrection of Christ, divides human time (days, months, years, centuries) like a directional arrow, connecting them both to the first day of creation and to the last day (the eighth) of the world, on which the Lord Jesus will come in glory and make all things new.

What is the relationship between Sunday and the liturgical year?

Sunday is the primordial feast, the foundation and core of the entire liturgical year, the natural model for understanding and celebrating, over the course of the liturgical year, the whole mystery of Christ, from the Incarnation and Nativity to the Ascension, to the day of Pentecost, and to the expectation in joyful hope of the Lord's return. Sunday, with its ordinary "solemnity," thus marks out, year by year, the time of the Church's pilgrimage, until the Sunday without any sunset. The Church, in fact, Sunday after Sunday, illuminated by Christ, marches toward the endless Sunday of the heavenly Jerusalem, when in the fullness of all its features will stand the mystical City of God, which "had no need of sun or moon to shine on it, for the glory of God gave it light, and its lamp was the Lamb" (Rev 21:23).

How is Sunday connected to our Baptism?

Sunday, the celebration of the Death and Resurrection of Christ, recalls better than the other days that we, with Christ and through him, died to sin and rose to the new life of the children of God precisely on the day of our Baptism. "You were buried with him in baptism, in which you were also raised with him through faith in the power of God, who raised him from the dead" (Col 2:12). The Church emphasizes this baptismal dimension of Sunday by urging that, apart from those celebrated on the Easter Vigil, Baptisms be celebrated on this day, Sunday, on which the Resurrection of the Lord is commemorated.

How is Sunday kept holy?

✠ Above all by participating in the Eucharistic celebration, which is truly, for every baptized person, the heart of Sunday. "Without Sunday we cannot live": thus proclaimed in 304 some of the Christians of Abitina (in present-day Tunisia), who suffered martyrdom under Diocletian precisely because they did not want to give up celebrating the Sunday Eucharist.

✠ And also through prayer, acts of charity, and abstaining from work.

How should Sunday Mass be lived?

✠ Sunday Mass is, for the Christian, an indispensable commitment to be lived not only to fulfill a precept, but as the need for a truly deliberate and consistent Christian life.

✠ The faithful assemble on Sunday because, listening to the Word of God and participating in the Eucharist, they commemorate the Passion, Resurrection, and glory of the Lord Jesus and give thanks to God who has regenerated them for a living hope by means of the Resurrection of Jesus Christ from the dead (see 1 Pt 1:3). At every Holy Mass, we bless the Lord, God of the universe, presenting him the bread and the wine, fruit of the earth and work of human hands.

✠ When parents participate with their children at Holy Mass, Christian families live out one of the most distinctive expressions of their identity and their "ministry" as domestic churches.

When is the Christian required to participate in Holy Mass?

"On Sundays and other holy days of obligation, the faithful are obliged to participate in the Mass" (CIC, c. 1247). Such a law implies a grave obligation, and it is easy to understand why if one considers the significance that Sunday and the Eucharist have for Christian life. Anyone who deliberately fails to fulfill this obligation commits a mortal sin.

Who can be exempted from participating in Sunday Mass?

Anyone who is justified by a serious reason (for example, illness) or has been exempted by his or her pastor.

How can Sunday be kept holy by praying more?

It is ideal for the Christian, in addition to participating in the Holy Mass, to keep Sunday holy by dedicating more time to prayer: personal, family, and community. These particular moments of prayer are for the Christian soul a preparation for and completion of the special gift of the Eucharist.

✠ Especially recommended is the solemn and communal celebration of Vespers. Ancient expressions of devotion, like pilgrimage, are also important. The faithful often take advantage of the Sunday respite to go shrines where they can experience, ideally with the whole family, a few hours of more intense faith and moments of grace.

✠ The time given to Christ is never lost, but is rather time gained for the profound humanization of our relationships, of our life and that of the world.

Why does keeping Sunday holy require rest, abstention from work?

✠ The alternation between work and rest, described in human nature, is willed by God himself, as shown in the passage on creation in the book of Genesis (see Gn 2:2-3; Ex 20:8-11). Rest is something "sacred," since it is needed in order for human beings to retreat from the sometimes excessively absorbing routine of worldly activities and be reminded that everything is the work of God. If on the first page of Genesis, the "work" of God is exemplary for human beings, so also is his "rest": "He rested on the seventh day from all the work he had undertaken" (Gn 2:2).

✠ The interruption of the often oppressive rhythm of occupations expresses, with the novelty of rest and detachment from work, a recognition of the dependence of oneself and of the cosmos on God. Everything is from God! The day of the Lord keeps coming back, over and over again, to affirm this principle. This recognition is all the more urgent in our time, in which science and technology have dramatically increased the power that human beings exercise through their work.

What are the advantages of the Sunday respite?

- Thanks to the Sunday respite, everyday concerns and tasks can regain their proper dimension.
- Material things, which so often cause agitation, give way for the values of the spirit.
- The people with whom we live recover, in a more serene encounter and dialogue, their true face. Rest and relaxation are necessary for our dignity as persons. The multiple and complementary demands of religion, family, culture, and relationships are hard to satisfy unless at least one day a week is set aside to enjoy together the possibility to rest and celebrate.

- The beauty of nature itself—too often ruined by a logic of domination that backfires against humanity—can be rediscovered and profoundly enjoyed.
- One can recover a bit of peace with God, with oneself, and with one's peers; a time suited for reflection, silence, study, and meditation, which foster the growth of the interior and Christian life.
- One can experience precious moments of spiritual enrichment, of greater freedom, of more possibilities for contemplation and fraternal communion. This requires every one of Christ's disciples to impart to other moments of the day as well, lived outside of the liturgical context—family life, social relations, entertainment—a style that encourages the emergence of the peace and joy of the Risen One in the ordinary fabric of life. The more tranquil disposition of parents and children can be, for example, an opportunity not only to open up for mutual communication but also to experience moments of growth and greater recollection.
- An opportunity is offered to dedicate oneself, with greater availability of time and energy, to activities of compassion, charity, and apostolate.

The Sunday Eucharist, therefore, not only does not detract from works of charity, but on the contrary, it impels the faithful all the more "to all the works of charity, piety, and the apostolate. For all these activities make it clear that Christ's faithful, though not of this world, are the light of the world and give glory to the Father in the sight of men" (*Sacrosanctum Concilium*, no. 9).

- Moments of fraternal sharing with the poorest of the poor are fostered. "On the first day of the week each of you should set aside and save whatever one can afford" (1 Cor 16:2) and give it to those who have less.

What kinds of work are permitted on Sunday?

Those that do not get in the way of offering worship to God and do not disrupt the joy proper to the Lord's Day or the rest that is due to mind and body. Family activities or activities that have great social utility are permitted unless they create habits that tend to compromise religion, family life, and health. Every Christian must also avoid unnecessarily imposing on others in a way that would prevent them from observing the Lord's Day.

What is the difference between Sunday and the "weekend"?

The disciples of Christ are asked not to confuse the celebration of Sunday, which must be a true sanctification of the Lord's Day, with the "weekend," fundamentally understood as a time of simple rest or distraction. Unfortunately, when Sunday loses its original significance and is reduced merely to the "weekend," it can happen that human beings remain closed within such a narrow horizon that they can no longer see "heaven."

Why is it important to keep Sunday holy by celebrating?

The need for "celebration" is inherent in human beings. Now for the Christian, Sunday, the day on which the Lord rose, is the day of joy par excellence. Sunday is rightly seen as a fulfillment of the Psalmist's acclamation, "This is the day the LORD has made; let us rejoice in it and be glad" (Ps 118:24). "On the first day of the week, you shall all rejoice," (cited in Pope John Paul II, *Dies Domini*) it says in the *Didascalia* of the apostles, from the earliest days of Christianity. On the Lord's Day, in fact, the Church gives powerful testimony to the joy that the apostles felt in seeing the risen Lord on the evening of Easter. "Voicing an awareness widespread in the Church, St. Augustine describes the joy of the weekly Easter: 'Fasting, is set aside and prayers are said standing, as a sign of the Resurrection, which is also why the Alleluia is sung on every Sunday'" (*Dies Domini*, no. 55). The festive character of the Sunday Eucharist expresses the joy that Christ transmits to his Church through the gift of the Spirit.

For more on this topic, see the following pontifical documents:

> Vatican Council II, *Sacrosanctum Concilium*
> John Paul II, *Dominicae Cenae* (1980); *Dies Domini* (1998)
> *Catechism of the Catholic Church*, nos. 2168-2195
> *Compendium of the CCC*, nos. 450-454

III
Sacred Images

What are religious images?

They are depictions of religious subjects, created with various materials and in different styles. In particular, they represent God, Jesus Christ, the Holy Spirit, the Blessed Mother, the saints.

What subjects are used in religious images?

Elements that come from this world, in their different components, are used: human, animal, vegetable, material. But these elements are depicted there to indicate something else: they point to realities that do not belong to this visible world. They are a reflection, a *sign* of the divine, of the religious, of the spiritual, of the supernatural.

What kind of transition is demanded by religious images?

In them, the human person is urged to pass from the visible to the invisible, from the signifying to the signified, from the created world to God. This is why we call religious images *symbolic*. They are a bridge between the visible and the invisible, between the believer and the mystery.

How long have religious images existed?

The decision to represent subjects of the Christian faith with images goes back a very long time. "Artists in every age have offered the principal facts of the mystery of salvation to the contemplation and wonder of believers by presenting them in the splendor of color and in the perfection of beauty" (*Compendium of the CCC*, Introduction).

Why do some religions prohibit religious images?

Judaism and Islam, for example, prohibit the depiction of God in that they want to emphasize the total invisibility, the infinite otherness and superiority of God with respect to his creatures: God is totally Other. The representation of the sacred in images constitutes a profanation for these religions.

Does the Old Testament prohibit images?

✠ In the Old Testament, God had ordered, "You shall not make for yourself an idol or a likeness of anything in the heavens above or on the earth below or in the waters beneath the earth" (Ex 20:4). This "divine injunction included the prohibition of every representation of God by the hand of man. Deuteronomy explains: 'Since you saw no form on the day that the Lord spoke to you at Horeb out of the midst of the fire, beware lest you act corruptly by making a graven image for yourselves, in the form of any figure. . . . ' It is the absolutely transcendent God who revealed himself to Israel. 'He is the all,' but at the same time 'he is greater than all his works.' He is 'the author of beauty.'

✠ "Nevertheless, already in the Old Testament, God ordained or permitted the making of images that pointed symbolically toward salvation by the incarnate Word: so it was with the bronze serpent, the ark of the covenant, and the cherubim" (CCC, nos. 2129-2130).

When were images prohibited in the history of Christianity?

✠ When there was iconoclasm, the religious movement that developed in the Byzantine empire between the eighth and ninth centuries, which considered devotion to sacred images (of Christ, the Virgin, the saints) idolatrous, and preached their destruction. The veneration of images (*iconolatria*) in the East had given rise to this fanaticism. The dispute became political when Byzantine Emperor Leo III the Isaurian, having decisively embraced iconoclasm (726), began to persecute the iconodules (devotees of images), closed rebellious monasteries and churches (confiscating their lands and distributing them to farmer-soldiers), and tried to impose the destruction of sacred images on Rome as well.

But the second Council of Nicaea in 787 decided in favor of images: "We define with all rigor and care that, like the depiction of the precious and life-giving Cross, so also the venerated and holy images, whether painted in mosaic or in any other suitable material, should be exposed in the holy churches of God, on the sacred furnishings, on the sacred vestments, on walls and on tables, in homes and in the streets; whether these be the image of the Lord God and our Savior Jesus Christ, or that of our immaculate Lady, the Holy Mother of God, of the holy angels, of all the saints and the just."

Images were reintroduced in the East starting in 843, when the Empress Theodora appointed Methodius as patriarch of Constantinople.

✠ After this, in the early sixteenth century, images were again prohibited, this time by Luther. But with a decree in 1563, the Council of Trent approved and justified devotion to images and condemned those who affirmed the contrary.

On what foundations are religious images based?

Religious images have various complementary foundations:

✠ Anthropological foundation
Being a union of body and soul, human beings express themselves through signs, words, gestures, and symbols. They perceive even spiritual realities through material signs and symbols. In the *Paradiso*, Dante affirms that the intellect cannot grasp the true nature of God without the sensory, or the mind can only grasp the sensory part that the intellect can then elaborate as it is.

✠ Sociological foundation

- As social beings, needing and desiring relationships with others, human beings need to communicate with others and do so by means of language, gestures, actions, and images.
- Moreover, we live today in a world that is particularly attentive to images, which have a particularly significant role in the life of the person and of society. It is not for nothing that the term *civilization of the image* is used to indicate modern society, and it is the reason why, today more than ever, in the civilization of the image, the sacred image can "express much more than what can be said in words, and be an extremely effective and dynamic way of communicating the Gospel message" (*Compendium of the* CCC, Introduction).

✠ Theological foundation

- There is a close relationship between the created world and God its Creator.

    In the Christian vision, the world was created by God, who wanted in this way to manifest and communicate his goodness, truth, and beauty. For this reason God speaks to human beings through the visible creation, which is a reflection, albeit limited, of the infinite perfection of God.
- Human beings were created in the image of God. Human beings are themselves the image of God. And therefore human beings are able to examine

themselves in order to know God: by getting to know themselves better as the image of God and by acting in keeping with this image, they know God better. And at the same time, it is just as true that by knowing God in his being and in his works, human beings also know themselves better.

- God has made himself visible in Jesus Christ. Since he is the Only-Begotten Son of God, intimately united with God the Father—"The Father and I are one" (Jn 10:30)—he allows us to know God the Father in a full, perfect, and definitive way: "Whoever has seen me has seen the Father" (Jn 14:9). Jesus Christ is the perfect visible image of the invisible God.

"Formerly, God, having no body or figure, could not in any way be represented by an image. But now that he has shown himself in the flesh and has lived among human beings, I can make an image of what I have seen of God" (St. John Damascene, *De Sacris Imaginibus Oratio*, 1, 16: PTS 17, 89, and 92).

So the Incarnation of Christ justifies the creation, possession, and veneration of religious images in Christianity.

Did Jesus use human signs and symbols to express the divine?

Jesus, in addition to being himself the One in whom God makes himself present and visible, often used, in his preaching and activity here on earth two thousand years ago, realities originating in creation in order to make known, proclaim, and communicate the mysteries of the Kingdom of God. One might also think of the symbolic meaning of his parables and miracles. Christ also used elements and signs from the world to institute the sacraments of the Church.

Are human images limited with respect to the divine?

We must certainly remember that no material image can ever fully express the ineffable mystery of God: the reality signified (religious, spiritual) always surpasses the human image. Nonetheless, the material element truly makes something of this mystery able to be glimpsed and perceived.

At the moment in which they become the vehicle of transmission for religious subjects, the profane aspects are grasped and represented in their positive aspects; but at the same time, they need to be purified, and above all supplemented and completed. And this takes place through the Christian subject matter that the images contain and transmit. In this sense, even popular myths and fables are taken up, purified, and transfigured by the Christian faith, in order to become religious images.

What is the purpose of religious images?

- Religious images facilitate access, comprehension, and transmission of content for persons belonging to different cultural, age, and language groups. They are easy to interpret and therefore reach a larger number of people than speech and writing.
- If they are seen, understood, interpreted, savored with the particular vision that comes from the Christian

faith, it is then possible to grasp the particular catechetical message that the artists wanted to transmit with the religious images.

In what sense do images have a catechetical purpose?

Since there is a strict correlation between the image and the symbol, and between the visible and the invisible world, it is logical and justified to proclaim the mystery of God by using symbolic images. This makes it possible to understand the blossoming, throughout the centuries, of Christian iconography, in which the evangelical and catechetical intention is accompanied by, or rather is closely interwoven with, the artistic and aesthetic aspect. The image is intended to transcribe the gospel message that Sacred Scripture transmits through the Word.

"The centuries-old conciliar tradition teaches us that images are also a preaching of the Gospel" (*Compendium of the CCC*, Introduction). Moreover, history teaches us that Christians, to proclaim the gospel message and catechize persons, have made special use of the *Biblia pauperum* ("Bible of the poor")—meaning images, visual catechisms, catechisms made up of images and of iconographic representations—even before written catechisms.

"Images and words are thus mutually enlightening. Works of art always 'speak,' at least implicitly, of the divine, of the infinite beauty of God, reflected in the Icon par excellence: Christ the Lord, the Image of the invisible God.

"Sacred images, with their beauty, are also a Gospel proclamation and express the splendor of the Catholic truth, illustrating the supreme harmony between the good and the beautiful, between the *via veritatis* and the *via pulchritudinis*. While they witness to the age-old and fruitful tradition of Christian art, they urge one and all, believers and non-believers alike, to discover and contemplate the inexhaustible fascination of the mystery of Redemption, giving an ever new impulse to the lively process of its inculturation in time" (Pope Benedict XVI, *Presentation of the* Compendium of the Catechism of the Catholic Church, June 28, 2005).

They are a particular form of popular catechesis, open books without words for all, a bridge between believer and mystery, while they adorn and decorate the sacred spaces, making them more welcoming and inviting for prayer.

Are images also an invitation to prayer?

Certainly. Christian art and iconography, in addition to being instruments at the service of evangelization and catechesis, have always been and still are an invitation to prayer: "The beauty and the color of the images are a stimulus for my prayer. It is a feast for my eyes, just as the view of the countryside opens my heart to give glory to God" (*De Sacris Imaginibus Oratio*, 1, 47). The contemplation of sacred images, together with listening to the Word of God, helps us to impress on our memories and hearts the mystery that we perceive, urging us to transform it into prayer and to bear witness to it in that newness of life that comes from the Christian faith and has its center in Christ.

What is the relationship between religious images and Christ?

The main purpose of all images in Christian iconography is the proclamation of the person, the message, the work of Christ, since he is the perfect Revealer of God the Father and the one definitive Savior of humanity and of the world. "The image of Christ is the liturgical icon *par excellence*. Other images, representations of Our Lady and of the Saints, signify Christ who is glorified in them" (*Compendium of the* CCC, no. 240), and, in proclaiming Christ, help us to foster faith in and love for him. Venerating the saints means recognizing that God is the source, the center, and the summit of their holiness. With the help of the Holy Spirit, the saints accepted the holiness of God in faith, and with docility they corresponded to this divine holiness with a holy life, following and imitating Christ, the image par excellence of the invisible God.

Because of this, when we enter into a church, we must first seek out the tabernacle where, if the tabernacle candle is lit, the Christ-Eucharist is present in a true, real, substantial way: Body, Blood, soul, and divinity. The homage of our greeting and our prayer must be addressed first of all to him, before and more so than to the images of the saints, images that instead are material representations.

What kind of devotion is given to images?

Not one of adoration (reserved solely for God), but of veneration.

Whom do we venerate in the image?

The Christian venerates

- Not the image in itself, which is simply a material object (a statue, an image, a symbol, a medal). If one were to venerate the object, one would fall into idolatry.
- The one whom the image is intended to represent, the "person" reproduced in the images: Jesus Christ, the Blessed Mother, the saints

In effect, "the honor paid to an image belongs to the one who is represented in it," and "the one who venerates the image venerates the reality of the one who is reproduced in it" (St. Basil the Great, *Liber de Spiritu Sancto*, 18, 45: SC 17b, 406). The honor paid to sacred images is a "respectful veneration," not an adoration appropriate only for God: "Acts of devotion are not directed to the images considered in themselves, but in that they serve to depict the incarnate God. Now, the motion that is made toward the image as image does not stop at it, but tends to the reality that it represents" (*Summa Theologiae*, II-II, q. 81, a. 3, ad 3).

How should sacred images be exposed in church?

The GIRM explains: "Images of the Lord, of the Blessed Virgin Mary, and of the Saints, in accordance with the most ancient tradition of the Church, should be displayed for veneration by the faithful and should be arranged so as to lead the faithful toward the mysteries of faith celebrated there. Care should, therefore, be taken that their number not be increased indiscriminately, and moreover that they be arranged in proper order so as not to draw the attention of the faithful to themselves and away from the celebration itself. There should usually be only one image of any given Saint. Generally speaking, in the ornamentation and arrangement of a church, as far as images are concerned, provision should be made for the devotion of the entire community as well as for the beauty and dignity of the images" (no. 318).

In what sense do religious images anticipate "new heavens" and a "new earth"?

Religious images, with their beauty and splendor, offer us an anticipation of the future reality: they present us with something that prefigures that transfiguration which, at the end of time, the whole world will one day receive from God. In fact, "After the final judgment the universe itself, freed from its bondage to decay, will share in the glory of Christ with the beginning of 'the new heavens' and a 'new earth' (2 Pt 3:13). Thus, the fullness of the Kingdom of God will come about, that is to say, the definitive realization of the salvific plan of God to 'unite all things in him, things in heaven and things on earth' (Eph 1:10). God will then be 'all in all' (1 Cor 15:28) in eternal life" (*Compendium of the* CCC, no. 216).

✠

For more on this topic, see the following pontifical documents:

Catechism of the Catholic Church, nos. 1145-1161
Compendium of the CCC, nos. 236-240
John Paul II, *Letter to Artists*, April 4, 1999

IV
Liturgical Vesture

A. The Festive Clothing of the Christian Faithful for the Celebration of the Sacraments

For many generations, Christians have used the best clothing, the most beautiful and well made, to participate in the various sacraments, in particular the celebration of the Sacraments of Baptism, the Eucharist—First Communion and Sunday Eucharist—and Marriage.

What is the religious significance of these garments?

These garments have various and complementary motivations, meanings, and purposes.

✠ Above all, it must be emphasized that the Church's liturgy reserves an important role for signs, and therefore also for the dress of the persons who participate in it. And this for different reasons:

- The liturgy is the summit and the source of the action of the Church and of the Christian, the first and necessary source from which to draw a truly Christian spirit. It is a celebration of the encounter with the living God in words and in images, in symbols and in gestures. The sense of the sacred in the liturgy is promoted above all by understanding more deeply the liturgical signs that characterize the various sacraments. These are above all and in the first place divine actions in words and signs, in human forms of expression. And it is important to point out this characteristic of the sacraments to the modern person, who is particularly attuned to symbols and signs and particularly receptive to the language of signs, in which the invisible is expressed in visible form.
- Liturgical worship involves the whole person: intellect, emotions, senses, soul, body, both the inner and outer dimension. The correct inner disposition required for serving God is also expressed in outward behavior and in clothing, in that the external elements contribute to reinforcing the internal attitudes, sentiments, and convictions.
- God is the Creator of heaven and earth, present in his work. All good things have God as their origin and end. This means that the material world, precious and good, is an important means through which God

manifests himself to human beings and human beings know and communicate with God.

✠ Festive garments express the faith and devotion of those who have commissioned and made them and of those who wear them. These garments, in addition to expressing, can also foster, feed, and reinforce the faith and devotion of all the participants in the sacramental celebrations, who are thus able to understand better the importance of the celebration even from the distinctive and festive dress of those present. In fact, not only what they hear, but also what they see counts a great deal. But a lack of proper attention to dress is an indication that faith is weak and that little importance is attributed to the action that is taking place.

✠ Particular care in the clothing that is used for the celebration of the sacraments expresses the distinction between sacred and profane in daily life. This distinction is particularly important in our time, in that a tendency is observed to eliminate the distinction between *sacrum* and *profanum*, given the widespread general tendency (at least in some places) toward the desacralization of everything. It is necessary instead to rediscover, emphasize, and respect the sacrality of the mystery of God, who makes himself present and acts in a special way in the sacraments, instituted by Christ and guarded and celebrated with devotion by the Church down through the centuries. It is therefore necessary to respect the character of *sacrum*, meaning the holy and sacred character of the sacrament to be celebrated, and in particular of the Eucharist, which is a holy and sacred action because the Christ, "the

Holy One" of God, is constantly present and active in it, and because it is constitutive of the sacred species (the Body and Blood of Christ), of the *sancta sanctis*, or holy things, Christ the Holy, given to the holy (the baptized faithful).

✠ The decoration and the beauty of the garments in liturgical celebrations express and recall the dignity and beauty of supernatural, heavenly realities. In fact:

- They manifest, although in limited fashion, the very beauty of God. Beauty is a fundamental dimension of human life. The human person is invited to grasp something of the infinite beauty of God, including through the beauty of liturgical dress.
- The divine gifts of the material world are molded by human hands into an expression of beauty that glorifies and praises the Creator.
- It is just and obligatory that we should always seek to offer the best and most beautiful things we have to God.
- In recent times, moreover, the *pulchrum* (the "beautiful") has emerged more and more as the way to arrive at God, the supreme Beauty, and to transmit to human beings something of the life of God, including through the artistic creation of garments.
- The solemnity and beauty of the garments, and in particular those worn on Sunday to participate in the Holy Mass, express a profound and penetrating sense of joy for our faith in the Resurrection of Christ. In fact, it was on a Sunday that Christ rose, and it is

therefore just and obligatory that this central event of the Christian faith should be celebrated with dignity, with joy, and in a festive atmosphere: these are elements that can and should show through even in the way that Christians dress in order to participate in the Eucharistic celebration on Sunday.

- The festive dress of the faithful anticipates and prefigures the deification of humanity, called to share at the end of time in heaven, for all eternity, in the resplendent life, the perfect joy, and the luminous glory of God: "They have washed their robes and made them white in the blood of the Lamb. 'For this reason they stand before God's throne and worship him day and night in his temple'" (Rev 7:14-15).

✠ Festive garments also help us to grasp the communal dimension inherent in every sacrament, which is always a celebration of the whole Church. In fact, since human beings have a nature that leads them to live together in society, they need perceptible expressions that will help them to live out this experience of community life. The garments worn by the participants at the celebration of a sacrament emphasize its communal and ecclesial, not solely individual, dimension. It is the festive celebration, not only of a whole family and parish community, but also of the whole Church, which shares in the joy of the individual.

B. The Vestments of the Priest for the Celebration of the Sacraments

What has already been said about the festive garments worn by the faithful when they participate in the celebration of the Christian sacraments also holds true for the liturgical vestments used by the priest in presiding over the celebration of the various sacraments.

But further reasons and purposes must be added that justify, in a specific way, the use of dignified liturgical vestments by the priest. And it is precisely for these specific and significant reasons that the vestments worn by priests, before being destined for liturgical use, are appropriately blessed.

What are the specific purposes of the liturgical vestments of the celebrating priest?

The liturgical vestments worn by the priest indicate the particular mission of the priest in the sacramental celebration. In every sacrament, he acts not simply as a man, but as a representative of Christ and as presider over the liturgical action, thanks to the special sacred power with which he is invested with the Sacrament of Holy Orders. The liturgical vestments that the celebrant wears therefore indicate the special ministerial service of the priest, who, by sacramental grace, does not celebrate in his own name or as the delegate of his community, but in his specific sacramental identification with the "supreme High Priest" who is Christ, *in persona Christi capitis* ("in the person of Christ the Head") and in the name of the Church. And the vestments that the priest wears remind him that he cannot consider himself an "owner" who is free to dispose of the liturgical text and the sacred rite as his own property, giving it his arbitrary personal style, but that he is acting in the name of an Other, fulfilling a mission that is essentially distinct from that of the other faithful.

In fact, "in the Church, which is the Body of Christ, not all members have the same function. This diversity of offices is shown outwardly in the celebration of the Eucharist by the diversity of sacred vestments, which must therefore be a sign of the function proper to each minister. Moreover, these same sacred vestments should also contribute to the decoration of the sacred action itself. The vestments worn by Priests and Deacons, as well as the attire worn by lay ministers, are blessed before being put into liturgical use according to the rite described in the Roman Ritual" (GIRM, no. 335).

What are the Church's guidelines on liturgical vestments?

✠ The subordination of the celebrating minister to the *mysterium*, which has been entrusted to him by the Church for the good of the entire People of God, must also find its expression in the observance of the liturgical requirements relative to the celebration of the various sacraments and of the Eucharist in particular. "These refer, for example, to dress, in particular to the vestments worn by the celebrant. Circumstances have of course existed and continue to exist in which the prescriptions do not oblige. We have been greatly moved when reading books written by priests who had been prisoners in extermination camps, with descriptions of Eucharistic Celebrations without the above-mentioned rules, that is to say, without an altar and without vestments. But although in those conditions this was a proof of heroism and deserved profound admiration, nevertheless in normal conditions to ignore the liturgical directives can be interpreted as a lack of respect towards the Eucharist, dictated perhaps by individualism or by an absence of a critical sense concerning current opinions, or by a certain lack of a spirit of faith" (Pope John Paul II, *Dominicae Cenae*, no. 12).

✠ Taking all of this into account, the Church has intervened to give appropriate guidelines on liturgical furnishings in general, and on sacred vestments in particular, in part for the sake of expressing as well as possible the religious and spiritual dimension of the sacramental celebration, avoiding every form of sensationalism or theatrical representation.

- "The ornamentation of a church should contribute toward its noble simplicity rather than to ostentation. Moreover, in the choice of elements attention should be paid to authenticity and there should be the intention of fostering the instruction of the faithful and the dignity of the entire sacred place ... Consequently, the Church constantly seeks the noble assistance of the arts and admits the artistic expressions of all peoples and regions. In fact, just as she is intent on preserving the works of art and the artistic treasures handed down from past centuries and, insofar as necessary, on adapting them to new needs, so also she strives to promote new works of art that are in harmony with the character of each successive age" (GIRM, no. 292).

"On account of this, in appointing artists and choosing works of art to be admitted into a church, what should be looked for is that true excellence in art which nourishes faith and devotion and accords authentically with both the meaning and the purpose for which it is intended" (GIRM, no. 289).

- "It is fitting that the beauty and nobility of each vestment not be sought in an abundance of overlaid ornamentation, but rather in the material used and in the design. Ornamentation on vestments should, moreover, consist of figures, that is, of images or symbols, that denote sacred use, avoiding anything unbecoming to this" (GIRM, no. 344).
- "In addition to traditional materials, natural fabrics proper to each region may be used, and also artificial fabrics that are in keeping with the dignity of the sacred action and the sacred person" (GIRM, no. 343).
- "As in the case of the building of churches, so also regarding all sacred furnishings, the Church admits the manner of art of each individual region and accepts those adaptations that are in keeping with the culture and traditions of the individual nations, provided that all are suited to the purpose for which the sacred furnishings are intended" (GIRM, no. 325).

- "In choosing materials for sacred furnishings, besides those which are traditional, others are admissible that, according to the mentality of our own age, are considered to be noble and are durable, and well suited for sacred use" (GIRM, no. 326).
- "As regards the form of sacred vestments, Conferences of Bishops may determine and propose to the Apostolic See adaptations that correspond to the needs and the usages of the individual regions" (GIRM, no. 342).

Down through the centuries, what has happened with liturgical vestments?

✠ In promoting the spiritual reform of the Church, St. Charles Borromeo also undertook a reform of the liturgy and urged the greatest attention and care in preparing, storing, and using liturgical vestments, ordering that those no longer fit be discontinued. Some of these were reused, others were destroyed.

✠ This is why we find fabrics from previous times incorporated into the vestments of subsequent periods. In certain circumstances, the fabrics were reused to make vestments in a new style, and the fabrics from previous eras, which seemed either too austere or too sumptuous with respect to the prevailing sensibility of that time period, became raw material to be reused in new forms.

What different kinds of liturgical vestments does the celebrant wear?

These are the main kind of liturgical vestments used by the priest for the celebration of the sacraments:

- The *amice*: A white piece of cloth worn around the neck when the alb does not completely cover the priest's ordinary dress.
- The *alb*: A vestment of white fabric that goes down to the ankles and completely covers the priest's clothing.
- The *cincture*: A cloth belt that cinches the alb around the celebrant's waist.
- The *stole*: An important emblem in the form of a scarf, worn around the priest's neck. The deacon wears it on a diagonal line from his left shoulder to his right hip.
- The *chasuble*: A vestment that the celebrant wears over the alb and the stole. It is made in the various liturgical colors.
- The *surplice*: An outer garment, often decorated with lace, that goes down to the knees, with short, wide sleeves, worn over the cassock. It is also used by altar servers.
- The *humeral veil*: A vestment worn over the shoulders for covering the monstrance as a sign of respect when the priest holds it during Eucharistic Benediction or during a procession or presentation of offerings.
- The *cope*: A liturgical vestment originally used for processions and afterward for the Liturgy of the

Hours on solemn feasts, the celebration of the sacraments outside of the Mass, and Benediction of the Most Holy Sacrament.

What are the liturgical colors for the celebration of the sacraments, and for the Holy Mass in particular?

✠ The colors emphasize the liturgical seasons and their particular characteristics: "Diversity of color in the sacred vestments has as its purpose to give more effective expression even outwardly whether to the specific character of the mysteries of faith to be celebrated or to a sense of Christian life's passage through the course of the liturgical year" (GIRM, no. 345).

✠ According to the kind and purpose of the celebration, the liturgical days and seasons of the Church year, the following colors are prescribed for the vestments: white, red, green, purple, pink, and black.

✠ In every period of the liturgical year, it is possible to replace the aforementioned colors with the color gold for particular reasons of solemnity.

✠ This is the liturgical period and the significance of each individual color:

- *White*: This is used in the seasons of Easter and Christmas, and on the feasts of the Blessed Mother and of saints who were not martyred. It is the color of Easter joy, of light and life.

- *Green*: This is used in ordinary time. It expresses the youthfulness of the Church, the resumption of a new life.
- *Red*: This is used on Palm Sunday, Good Friday, Pentecost, and on the feast days of the martyrs. It signifies the gift of the Holy Spirit, who makes us capable of witnessing to our faith even to the point of martyrdom. (It also symbolizes blood.)
- *Purple*: This is used during Advent, Lent, and in liturgies for the deceased. It symbolizes hope, the anticipation of meeting Jesus, the spirit of penance, and Christian hope in moments of suffering and sorrow.
- *Pink*: This is used only in the Roman Rite for the Third Sunday of Advent and for the Fourth Sunday of Lent. It indicates the anticipation of the approaching solemnity.
- *Black*: This is sometimes used in funerals and in celebrations for the deceased.

For more on this topic, see the following pontifical documents:

John Paul II, *Dominicae Cenae*, no. 12

General Instruction of the Roman Missal, nos. 289-335, 390, 342-345

Congregation for Divine Worship and the Discipline of the Sacraments, *Redemptionis Sacramentum*, March 25, 2004

V
Why Baptize Babies?

What is Baptism?

✠ It is

- One of the Seven Sacraments instituted by Jesus Christ
- The source of all Christian life
- The door that opens access to all the other sacraments
- The foundation of communion among all Christians

✠ The essential Rite of Baptism consists in the immersion of the candidate in water, or the pouring of water over his or her head, together with the invocation of the Most Holy Trinity: Father, Son, and Holy Spirit.

What objections are raised against infant Baptism?

Various objections are raised concerning infant Baptism, but this is not an entirely recent development. These objections have been summarized in the *Instruction on Infant Baptism* from the Congregation for the Doctrine of the Faith:

✠ "Many parents are distressed to see their children abandoning the Faith and no longer receiving the sacraments, in spite of their own efforts to give them a Christian upbringing, and some pastors are asking themselves whether they should not be stricter before admitting infants to Baptism. Some think it better to delay the Baptism of children until the completion of a catechumenate of greater or less duration, while others are asking for a re-examination of the teaching on the necessity of Baptism, at least for infants, and wish the celebration of the sacrament to be put off until such an age when an individual can make a personal commitment, perhaps even until the beginning of adult life" (no. 2).

✠ "In view of the link between the person and society, some people hold that infant Baptism is still suitable in the homogeneous type of society, in which values, judgments and customs form a coherent system; but they hold that it is inappropriate in today's societies, which are characterized by instability of values and conflicts of ideas. In the present situation, they say Baptism should be delayed until the candidate's personality has sufficiently matured" (no. 23).

✠ "A final criticism of infant Baptism would have it that the practice comes from a pastoral usage lacking missionary impetus and concerned more with administering a sacrament than with stirring up faith and fostering commitment to spreading the Gospel. It is asserted that, by retaining infant Baptism, the Church is yielding to the temptation of numbers and social establishment, and that she is encouraging the maintenance of a magical concept of the sacraments, while she really ought to engage in missionary activity, bring the faith of Christians to maturity, foster their free conscious commitment, and consequently admit a number of stages in her sacramental pastoral practice" (no. 25).

What are the reasons in favor of infant Baptism?

✠ There are many reasons that justify, even today, the practice of baptizing infants. These reasons

- Are not to be considered in isolation, but in conjunction with one another. In this way they offer, like the tiles of a mosaic, an elaborate justification of the doctrine and practice of the Church.
- Appear intimately connected and in profound harmony both with the fundamental contents of the Christian faith and with essential dimensions (values) of the human person

✠ The main reasons are

- The ancient practice of the Church
- The gratuitous initiative of God
- The importance of holiness

- Faith as birth/new life (with its liberating and communitarian characteristics)
- The dignity of the infant
- The role of the parents
- The mission of the Church

Is the practice of baptizing infants recent or ancient?

✠ In the Church, the practice of baptizing both adults and children is an ancient one.

✠ Baptizing infants constitutes an immemorial practice both in the East and in the West.

- Origen, and later St. Augustine, maintained that it was a "tradition received from the apostles."
- The most ancient known ritual, from the beginning of the second century, presents the apostolic tradition as follows: "First baptize the children. Those of them who can speak for themselves should do so. The parents or someone of their family should speak for the others" (*Instruction on Infant Baptism*, no. 4, citing *La Tradition apostolique de Saint Hippolyte*, eds. and trans. B. Botte, Munster, Aschendorff [*Liturgiewissenschafliche Quellen und Forschungen* 39, 1963], 44).
- This practice has been reiterated, supported, and justified repeatedly by popes, councils, synods, down to Paul VI, who quite rightly recalled the age-old teaching on this point, affirming that "Baptism should be conferred even on infants who are yet unable to commit any sin personally, in order that, having been

born without supernatural grace, they may be born again of water and the Holy Spirit to divine life in Christ Jesus" (cited in CDF, *Instruction on Infant Baptism*, no. 8).

What are the characteristics of God's action in infant Baptism?

God's action in the Sacrament of Baptism conferred upon infants is a gratuitous, anticipatory action, which does not presuppose human merit.

✠ God grants a very special gift to children before they are able to deserve it in any way. The pure gratuitousness of the gift of God is manifested in an entirely particular way in infant Baptism.

✠ This gratuitous gift of God is a very rich reality, which includes

- The remission of Original Sin and of all personal sins
- Sanctifying grace, which makes the baptized person capable of believing in God and of living under the influence of the Holy Spirit
- Birth to new life, through which the person becomes an adopted child of the Father, a member of Christ, a temple of the Holy Spirit
- Participation in the priesthood of Christ, through which the baptized person offers his or her own life as a spiritual sacrifice "pleasing to God" (1 Pt 2:5)

- Incorporation into the Church, the Body of Christ, and participation in its mission of proclaiming, celebrating, and bearing witness to Christ the Lord
- The bestowal of the theological virtues (faith, hope, charity) and the gifts of the Holy Spirit
- The conferral on the soul of an indelible spiritual sign, the character that consecrates the baptized person for the worship of the Christian religion. Because of the character that it imparts, Baptism cannot be repeated.

✠ "No one can enter the kingdom of God without being born of water and Spirit" (Jn 3:5). These words of the Gospel manifest the anticipatory love of a God-Father who invites all of his children to participate in his life: the self-donation of God through Christ in the Spirit.

✠ Baptismal life thus becomes "doxology," the praise and glorification of the Most Holy Trinity, for the salvation of the world.

✠ Baptized children remind us that the missionary fecundity of the Church has its life-giving roots not in human means but in the absolutely gratuitous gift of God.

✠ The Sign of the Cross itself, which concludes the Rite of Baptism, indicates among other things that the Triune God takes anticipatory and gratuitous possession of the person, who is consecrated to Christ.

How does infant Baptism emphasize the importance of holiness?

✠ Holiness is an essential and inseparable component of the new life of Baptism, and is therefore a constitutive element of the dignity of the person.

✠ The baptized child bears witness to being holy already, as a child of God (by a gratuitous gift of God) and, at the same time, not yet being fully holy (an aspect that requires efforts of conversion, penance, and everyday conduct).

In this way, children, made holy through Baptism, become capable of a specific apostolic action in the Church. They become active subjects, authentic witnesses and collaborators, in the communion of the saints, of the Church's growth in holiness.

✠ Moreover, the Lord Jesus gives his delicate and generous love to children, reserving his blessing for them, assuring them the Kingdom of Heaven (see Mt 19:13-15; Mk 10:14), pointing them out as a model (see Mt 18:3-5; "Whoever humbles himself like this child is the greatest in the kingdom of heaven").

✠ This is a recognition of the fact that even during infancy and childhood, there are valuable opportunities for the edification of the Church and the humanization of society.

✠ In this context, a statement from Vatican Council II, in *Gaudium et Spes*, seems more important and relevant than ever: "Children contribute in their own way to making their parents holy" (no. 48). In fact, if it is true that children are as they are raised by their parents (who are parents by virtue of the fact that they have children!), it is just as true that during the entire time that they are raising their children, parents are changing, growing, being shaped in both human and supernatural terms, thanks to the work of training provided by the children themselves.

✠ The invocation of the saints in the Rite of Baptism, while it solicits the protection of those who have already brought their baptismal journey to a happy conclusion, at the same time expresses the intimate communion that unites the baptized, who in every age make holiness their program and model of life.

In what way does infant Baptism manifest as birth/new life?

✠ St. Gregory of Nissa says of this, "The new offspring conceived by means of the faith comes to birth through the regeneration of Baptism, has the Church as mother, sucks the milk of its doctrine and its institutions."

For his part, St. Augustine appeals to the baptized in these words: "Let us rejoice and give thanks: we have become not only Christians but Christ himself . . . Marvel and rejoice, for we have become Christ" (*In Ioann. Evang. Tract.* 21:8, CCL 36:216).

✠ Baptism is the beginning of this spiritual, supernatural birth/new life of the believer in Christ. Confirmation is its reinforcement, and the Eucharist is its nourishment.

✠ "Born with a fallen human nature and tainted by original sin, children also have need of the new birth in Baptism to be freed from the power of darkness and brought into the realm of the freedom of the children of God, to which all men are called" (CCC, no. 1250).

✠ Nor must one underestimate the anthropological value, present in all the religions, of celebrating in some way the salient and emblematic moments of life—birth, the passage to adulthood, marriage, death—with culturally and socially determined rituals, which incorporate both a more or less well-defined reference to the "sacred" and an aspect of social integration.

✠ Water, the material of the Sacrament of Baptism, appears in the biblical texts as

- Prime matter, primordial and fundamental element of the birth/life of the world, principle of creation, and therefore a sign of the new creation made by God, through Christ, in the Spirit
- A sign of the birth of the new messianic age, realized with Christ
- The source of life and fecundity
- A symbol of death. Precisely through this symbolism, Baptism signifies communion in the Death of Christ; the baptized person is buried with him and raised with him: "Are you unaware that we who were baptized into Christ Jesus were baptized into his death? We were indeed buried with him through baptism

into death, so that, just as Christ was raised from the dead by the glory of the Father, we too might live in newness of life" (Rom 6:3-4).

What kind of life is exemplified in infant Baptism?

✠ A generated life. Infant Baptism, in fact, highlights the relationship between human generation and generation in the faith. The Church, as a mother, generates to the faith and in the faith. St. Augustine wrote in this regard, "When children are presented to be given spiritual grace, it is not so much those holding them in their arms who present them—although, if these people are good Christians, they are included among those who present the children—as the whole company of saints and faithful Christians . . . It is done by the whole of Mother Church which is in the saints, since it is as a whole that she gives birth to each and every one of them" (Epist. 98, 5: PL 33, 362, cited in *Instruction on Infant Baptism*, no. 14).

✠ A life that grows.

- Precisely the fact that Baptism is the first but not the only Sacrament of Christian Initiation, which combines with Confirmation and the Eucharist to constitute the full Christian identity, highlights the dynamic nature of Christian life, a life in constant growth toward the fullness of maturity in Christ. The three Sacraments of Initiation are so intimately connected to each other that they lead the faithful to that Christian maturity through which they may accomplish, in the Church and in the world, the mission proper to the People of God.

- Baptism is at the same time a dynamic point of departure. Once baptized, the constant task is that of understanding and embodying one's baptismal dignity more and more, heeding the admonition of St. Leo the Great: "*Agnosce, o christiane, dignitatem tuam*"; "Christian, recognize your dignity." Or that of St. Maximus, bishop of Turin, to those who had received the anointing of Baptism: "Consider the honor that is bestowed on you in this mystery."

- In the rediscovery of the gift and reality of Baptism, there is a steady growth of the fundamental attitude of discipleship and witness, which "immerses" itself more and more in Christ died and risen, and expresses itself in the complete profession of the faith and in the sacramental fraternity of the Church, just as Christ wanted it to be.

- "For the grace of Baptism to unfold, the parents' help is important. So too is the role of the *godfather* and *godmother*, who must be firm believers, able and ready to help the newly baptized—child or adult—on the road of Christian life. Their task is a truly ecclesial function (*officium*). The whole ecclesial community bears some responsibility for the development and safeguarding of the grace given at Baptism" (CCC, no. 1255).

What dimensions of the faith appear in infant Baptism?

Infant Baptism highlights the liberating and communitarian dimensions of the faith.

✠ The liberating dimension of the faith:

- Through Baptism, the person is offered the possibility of being freed, from the very first days of life, from Original Sin, participating in the filial divine life in a holy and immaculate way.
- Baptizing infants therefore confirms the Church's faith in the reality of Original Sin, which takes hold of the person from birth. The Council of Carthage in 418 condemned "those who deny that children should be baptized as soon as they come from the mother's womb" and emphasized that "even the youngest, who have not yet been able to commit any sin personally, are truly baptized for the remission of sins, so that through regeneration what they have received from birth may be purified in them."
- "Water is what the flesh is immersed in so that all of its sins may be washed away. In it all shame is buried" (St. Ambrose).
- So even from birth there begins that "fight against evil, that dying to sin" that sets apart the life of the baptized person and leads him or her to share in the Resurrection of Christ.

✠ The communitarian dimension of the faith:

- "For in one Spirit we were all baptized into one body" (1 Cor 12:13); "One body and one Spirit . . . one Lord, one faith, one baptism" (Eph 4:4-5).
- It is in the faith of the whole Church, made present in the liturgical assembly, that children are baptized. "They are baptized," we read in the Introduction to the *Rite of Baptism for Children*, "in the faith of the Church, a faith proclaimed for them by their parents and godparents, who represent both the local Church and the whole society of saints and believers" (no. 2). Baptism is administered to children on account of the faith of the Church, and not simply that of the parents (see *Pastoralis Actio*, 14, in EV 7/600). At the same time, the Church wisely demands the guarantee that "once baptized, the child will receive the Christian upbringing required by the sacrament; it must have a well-founded hope that the baptism will bear its fruit" (ibid., no. 30).
- This leads to the recommendation in the Introduction that Baptism, the doorway and foundation of communion in the Church, normally be celebrated in the parish church on a Sunday and at a time that allows the community to be present, "so that baptism may clearly appear as the sacrament of the Church's faith and of incorporation into the people of God" (no. 10).
- And therefore the baptized child must be brought up in the faith and to the faith of the Church, in order to realize fully the reality of the sacrament.

How is the dignity of the child manifested in infant Baptism?

The conferral of Baptism on children emphasizes the dignity of being a child, prior to and above his or her role in life.

✠ Contemporary society focuses most of its attention on doing, on working, on roles, on efficiency. This creates a risk, neither remote nor circumscribed, of not sufficiently appreciating the child in his or her personal dignity. This dignity, in fact, requires that the person be considered not in light of what he or she does, but first of all and above all for what he or she is. If activity is used as the measuring stick, the child is in danger of being seen as useless and incapable solely as a function of others (adults, parents), or at most is appreciated for his or her latent potential that will bear fruit in the future.

✠ Baptism, administered to a person who is such "long before it can show it by acts of consciousness and freedom" (*Instruction on Infant Baptism*, no. 20), emphasizes before a utilitarian and efficiency-driven society such as ours the importance and the dignity of the child's personhood.

✠ "The human being is to be respected and treated as a person from the moment of conception; and therefore from that same moment his rights as a person must be recognized, among which in the first place is the inviolable right of every innocent human being to life" (*Donum Vitae*, no. 1). The text is speaking of human life here, of course, but why couldn't this right also be applied to divine life, which neither diminishes nor takes anything away from human life, but on the contrary fulfills and elevates it through supernatural filial adoption?

☩ With the awareness that true "worship of God" consists in offering oneself, one's own life "as a living sacrifice, holy and pleasing to God" (see Rom 12:1-2), one understands how the very life of the child can truly constitute such "worship of God."

☩ The imposition of the name at the beginning of the Rite of Baptism is an expression, a sign of this original and unrepeatable dignity of each child, which is due to

- The fact that God knows and loves each one individually
- The unique and irreplaceable role that every Christian has from God in the salvific plan of the Church and of the history of humanity
- The call to respond with an openness commensurate with the gift of intimate filial communion from a God who knows and loves us individually

This is why it is important that the name given to the child be that of a saint, who can be a lifelong model for the baptized person as well as an intercessor and protector.

☩ The conferral of the white garment in the baptismal rite is another sign of the new dignity acquired by the baptized person, who, as a new person, has put on Christ, already participating in a certain way in his glory, anticipated in the Transfiguration ("and his clothes became white as light," Mt 17:2) and fulfilled in the Resurrection, and acquiring the right to participate, wearing the required wedding garment, in the banquet of the heavenly bridegroom (see Mt 17:1f.).

What is the role of the parents in infant Baptism?

Infant Baptism places tremendous importance on the role of the parents and of the family in general (not to mention other relatives, through the godparents). In fact:

✠ The parents are already involved in the period before Baptism: in fact, they freely ask for it, prepare for the celebration . . . Their presence and active participation at the moment of celebration is also strongly recommended. This is why it is asked that the Baptism be celebrated as soon as the mother of the child to be baptized is also able to participate in the rite.

✠ In the post-baptismal period, their work of child raising appears indispensable for the Christian maturation of the baptized child.

✠ At the same time, the Church, in not admitting children to Baptism without the consent of their parents and their explicit commitment to guarantee a serious Christian education for the baptized child, shows that it recognizes and respects both the natural rights of the parents and the child's need to grow in faith.

✠ At the same time, the right and duty of parents to give their children what they believe to be good for them must be recognized and proclaimed, just as it is their right and duty to raise their children as they think is best. It is therefore an indispensable requirement that Christian parents share with their children, as soon as they are born, the unique and essential gift that they have received from God, which is faith and Baptism.

✠ This right and duty, made explicit by Vatican Council II in the declaration *Dignitatis Humanae*, was affirmed on an international level by the *Universal Declaration of Human Rights* (art. 26, no. 3). Now for Christian parents who truly consider themselves such, what could be greater and more sublime than participation in the divine life, to be transmitted as a most precious gift to their children?

✠ If the children, after growing up, should unfortunately abandon the Christian faith, this would not mean that the Christian upbringing provided by their parents was pointless: at the very least, it taught the children the faith (we hope in its genuine and authentic form) that they now reject, and has therefore made them more aware of and responsible for this rejection.

How is the mission of the Church expressed in infant Baptism?

Infant Baptism highlights the Church's mission in various ways:

✠ The faith of the individual needs the community of believers. It is only in the faith of the Church that each of the faithful is able to believe.

✠ Christ has given his Church, which he himself founded, the command, "Go, therefore, and make disciples of all nations, baptizing them in the name of the Father, and of the Son, and of the holy Spirit" (Mt 28:19). So children too, who were the object of a special love on the part of Christ himself ("Let the children come to me," Mk 10:14; "Unless you turn and become like children," Mt 18:3), are recipients of the Church's mission.

✠ Through its doctrine and practice, the Church has demonstrated that it knows no means other than Baptism to guarantee children access to eternal beatitude.

Who can administer Baptism?

✠ The ordinary ministers of Baptism are the bishop and priest and, in the Latin Church, the deacon. In case of necessity, anyone can baptize, on the condition that he or she intends to do what the Church does and pours water over the head of the candidate, saying, "I baptize you in the name of the Father, and of the Son, and of the Holy Spirit."

The Church finds the justification for the possibility that anyone can baptize in the universal salvific will of God and in the necessity of Baptism for salvation.

If the child to be baptized is in danger of dying, Baptism must be celebrated as soon as possible: "This is licit even when the parents are opposed and even when the infant is the child of non-Catholic parents" (*Rite of Baptism*, Introduction, no. 8).

✠ What is called the "Baptism of desire" is also important: this is the Baptism that the Christian mother, as soon as she knows she is pregnant, desires for the child she is carrying in her womb. This Baptism has the effects of Baptism, even if the sacrament is not celebrated.

What about children who die without Baptism?

✠ As for the children who die without Baptism, the liturgy of the Church invites us to entrust them to the mercy of God.

✠ At the same time, the Church affirms its hope of salvation for children who have died without receiving Baptism. It bases this hope on

- The universal salvific will of God
- The universality of the sole mediation of Christ
- The tenderness of Jesus toward children, which led him to say, "Let the children come to me; do not prevent them." (Mk 10:14)
- The primacy of divine grace
- The sacramentality of the Church

✠ The Church offers help and consolation to those who have suffered the death of an unbaptized child.

✠

For more on this topic, see the following pontifical documents:

Catechism of the Catholic Church, nos. 1213-1284
Compendium of the CCC, nos. 252-264
Congregation for the Doctrine of the Faith, *Instruction on Infant Baptism*, 1980
International Theological Commission, *The Hope of Salvation for Infants Who Die Without Being Baptized*, 2007

VI
When and How to Confess

First of all, what is the Sacrament of Confession?

The Sacrament of Confession (or of Penance, or of Reconciliation) is the celebration of the merciful love of God, who gives us forgiveness of our sins through the Death and Resurrection of Christ, who, through the ministry of the Church, reconciles us with God and with our brothers and sisters.

Confessing therefore means

- Listening to the Word of God and recognizing our sins
- Celebrating the merciful love of God the Father, who
  - Forgives our sins, washing them in the Blood of his Son
  - Communicates to us his own divine life (sacramental grace)

- Reconciles us with him and among ourselves, restoring our bond of universal fellowship
- Embraces and empowers our personal commitment of continual conversion inaugurated with Baptism and punctuated by the demands of the Eucharistic celebration
- Opens our repentant hearts to the breath of the Holy Spirit, who leads us to justice, charity, freedom, life, and joy

Who instituted this sacrament?

It was instituted by Jesus Christ, when on the evening of Easter he showed himself to his apostles and said to them: "Receive the holy Spirit. Whose sins you forgive are forgiven them, and whose sins you retain are retained" (Jn 20:22-23).

Why is confession necessary?

Because every Christian, after Baptism, commits a sin.

And what if someone claims to be without sin?

He or she is either lying or blind. "If we say, 'We are without sin,' we deceive ourselves, and the truth is not in us" (1 Jn 1:8).

When is a sin committed?

✠ When we disobey God, his love, the law he has given to us through Christ to show us the right way toward our full happiness and the perfect realization of our being: holiness.

"I have done what is evil in your eyes" (Ps 51:6).

✠ In particular, we realize that we have sinned in the light of Christ. It is Christ, in fact, with his Word and his Death and Resurrection, who fully reveals to us our sins and their gravity.

In what sense does sin offend God?

✠ Sin offends God in the sense that it

- Wounds or destroys the person whom God has created and loves
- Disrupts or interrupts the dialogue between God and the person
- Rejects his Word (law, teachings, etc.), which is the true good of the person
- Offends God not so much in his honor as in his love, as Creator and Father

In what sense does sin damage the person who commits it?

Sin is harmful in that the sinner, by rejecting God and his teachings, rejects the highest and only good, the source of full happiness.

Are all sins equal?

Certainly not. Sins differ, for example, by seriousness and kind.

- ✠ As for gravity, there are sins that are

  - Mortal: "There is such a thing as deadly sin." (1 Jn 5:16)
  - Venial

- ✠ As for kind, there are sins

  - Of thought, word, act, omission
  - Against God, neighbor, ourselves, creation

When is a mortal sin committed?

In order to commit a mortal sin, three conditions have to be met at the same time:

- Grave matter
- Full knowledge
- Deliberate consent

Who determines what is grave matter?

It is God (and not us or the people . . .) who determines what is grave matter. God indicates this in particular through the Ten Commandments and teachings of Christ, reiterated by his Church.

When is a venial sin committed?

When grave matter is not involved, or, even if grave matter is involved, there is not full knowledge or deliberate consent.

Is it enough to ask for God's forgiveness on one's own, without the Sacrament of Confession?

✠ Every one of us can and should ask for God's forgiveness at every moment, especially immediately after every mortal sin and before going to bed at night, as also at the beginning of the celebration of the Holy Mass.

✠ But God forgives some of our sins—mortal sins—when we come with repentance to the Sacrament of Confession, willed and instituted by his Son Jesus Christ. God has shown us how he intends to grant us his forgiveness. Of course, sin is not forgiven if there is no personal repentance, but God has made the remission of sins dependent on the ecclesial ministry, or at least on the serious intention to seek it out as soon as possible, when there is not an immediate opportunity to make a sacramental confession.

How often should one go to confession?

✠ Every Christian, after reaching the age of reason, is required to go to confession at least once a year.

✠ But the good Christian cannot and must not settle for the minimum requirement. In particular, the good Christian

- In the case of a mortal sin: must go to confession immediately after committing a mortal sin, in order to obtain God's forgiveness immediately and avoid hell in case of death. And in any case, he or she must confess before receiving Holy Communion.

A complete individual confession and absolution constitute the only ordinary way in which the Christian who is aware of having committed mortal sin is reconciled with God and with the Church.

- In the case of venial sins: if one has committed only venial sins, the time that can pass between one confession and the other depends on the person's own spiritual sensibility.

Certain saints confessed every day, and they were saints! Following the suggestion of good spiritual Fathers, it would be appropriate for a Christian who has not committed mortal sins to confess once a month, or every two months at the least, especially if he or she receives Holy Communion frequently.

Why is the frequent confession of even venial sins so highly recommended?

✠ It is ideal to make habitual, humble, and trusting recourse to the Sacrament of Penance, because this sacrament

- Increases grace
- Strengthens the virtues
- Helps to mitigate the negative tendencies inherited on account of Original Sin and aggravated by personal sins
- Forms an upright conscience
- Offers the gift of serenity and peace by the very fact that it increases grace

✠ One should also not forget the importance of the Penitential Rite that is found at the beginning of the Eucharistic celebration, in which the faithful ask for God's forgiveness for their sins.

How do we make a confession?

✠ First of all, we prepare for the celebration of the sacrament with moments of prayer and with good spiritual direction.

✠ We then confront ourselves with the example and words of Christ (examination of conscience), preferably while reading a passage of Sacred Scripture.

✠ In the light of what God has done for us, we recognize our sins, asking God for forgiveness and making a commitment to "change our lives," especially in one particular area (resolution).

✠ We then go to the priest (beginning by saying how long it has been since our last confession and concluding by saying that we also intend to confess the sins that we do not remember and those of our past).

- We confess our sins.
- We listen to the words of the priest.
- We accept the penance that is given.
- We express our repentance, motivated above all by love for God, and recite the Act of Contrition (or a similar formula).

- With faith, we receive absolution: "I absolve you from your sins in the name of the Father, and of the Son, and of the Holy Spirit."

✠ We then thank the Lord for the sacramental gift that we have received, renewing our commitment to conversion of life.

Is it enough to make a generic accusation of our sins?

✠ No, it is not enough. Any practice that would limit confession to a generic accusation (for example, saying, "Father, I have sinned, please give me absolution . . .") or to confessing only a few sins believed to be the most significant, is not to be tolerated.

✠ The Christian is obligated to confess, according to their kind and number, all mortal sins committed after Baptism and not yet revealed in confession, as made known after a diligent examination of conscience.

Should confession be done behind the screen or not?

The *Code of Canon Law* says in this regard: "The conference of bishops is to establish norms regarding the confessional; it is to take care, however, that there are always confessionals with a fixed grate between the penitent and the confessor in an open place so that the faithful who wish to can use them freely" (c. 964 §2). So the penitent must be guaranteed the possibility of using the screen and must also be the one who decides whether or not to use it, not the confessor.

How is a diligent examination of conscience made?

✠ By allowing ourselves to be illuminated by the Word of God (the Bible). In fact, it is the Word of God that

- Reveals sin
- Calls to conversion
- Urges the practice of virtue
- Encourages the imitation of Christ
- Proclaims the mercy of God, who washes sin away with the Blood of Christ and gives the grace of the Holy Spirit, who sanctifies the human person

✠ In particular, we can make a good examination of conscience by reviewing the Ten Commandments, the Beatitudes, or the precepts of this Church (see in this regard the section "Forming Conscience").

Is it possible to confess during the Holy Mass?

✠ Yes, it is possible, but it would be better to confess beforehand, or in any case outside of the Holy Mass, since it is not possible to celebrate two sacraments well at the same time. The celebration of confession during the Mass creates an overlapping that ends up damaging these two events of salvation, genuine pillars of the Christian life, each of which therefore needs a specific time of celebration.

✠ The faithful are therefore recommended to approach the Sacrament of Penance outside of the celebration of the Mass, choosing a moment of calm for themselves and for the confessor so that this sacrament may be celebrated well.

Is the confessor always bound to secrecy?

Of course, without any exceptions and under very severe penalties. He must maintain absolute secrecy (the sacramental seal) about the sins confessed by his penitents, even if his life is at stake.

Can everyone receive absolution?

✠ Penitents who are living in a habitual state of mortal sin (for example, those who have divorced and remarried) and do not intend to change their situation cannot validly receive absolution.

✠ In any case, sin is not forgiven if there is no personal repentance and the intention to sin no more.

✠ Some particularly serious sins, which are punished with excommunication, can be solved only by the pope or by the bishop, or by priests delegated by them.

✠ In the case of imminent danger of death, any priest can absolve from any sin or excommunication.

What is the relationship between this celebration of the Sacrament of Confession and everyday life?

The celebration of the sacramental Rite of Penance is closely connected to everyday life. By confessing, one makes the commitment, before the community and before God, to walk once again according to the fundamental Christian choice, to do everything that Christ proposed as the way to the true and definitive liberation of the human person, for full and joyful communion with God and with one's brothers and sisters. "You have had yourselves washed, you were sanctified, you were justified in the name of the Lord Jesus Christ and in the Spirit of our God" (1 Cor 6:11). So walk in new life.

"This is the will of God, your holiness" (1 Thes 4:3).

For more on this topic, see the following pontifical documents:

Rite of Penance, 1974

Pope John Paul II, *Reconciliatio et Paenitentia*, 1985

Catechism of the Catholic Church, nos. 1420-1484; 1846-1876

Compendium of the CCC, nos. 296-312; 391-400

VII
Forming Conscience

A. Preliminary Questions

How long has it been since you made a good confession? The last time, did you confess all of the serious sins you had committed? In past confessions, did you ever intentionally fail to mention any mortal sins? How long has it been since you received Communion? Have you always received it in the proper state? Have you ever gone to Communion with mortal sins on your conscience, without confessing beforehand? Have you ever profaned the Eucharist by committing a sacrilege? Have you failed to respect the Most Holy Sacrament by approaching Communion without observing the prescribed fast, talking, laughing, without preparation, and without thinking about whom you were about to receive? Do you do penance on Fridays? Do you know how to live abstinently, especially on the days commanded by the Church? Have you eaten meat on Fridays during Lent? Have you fasted on Ash Wednesday and Good Friday? Have you help the Church by donating to its works (missions, seminaries, support for the clergy, etc.)?

B. Questions About the Ten Commandments

1. You shall not have other gods beside me.

Do you believe in God, the Father and Savior of yourself and of all? Is your life oriented to God? Do you love him like a child? Have you put him in first place among the values of your life? Do you believe in the Father, the Son, and the Holy Spirit? Do you pray in the morning and the evening? Do you live the Christian virtues of faith, hope, and charity? Do you consider the faith a precious gift to be cultivated? Do you make an effort to grow in the faith? Are you convinced of your Catholic religion? Do you seek and accept the will of God throughout your day, especially in difficult moments? Have you endangered your faith by reading books, magazines, or articles contrary to the faith, to Christ, to the Church? Do you try to know, to explore, and to understand the truths of the Christian faith? Have you spoken poorly of religion, the pope, or priests? Have you driven anyone away from religious practice? Do you hope in the love of God, or are you discouraged and despairing in the face of the difficulties of life, cursing and rebelling? Are you superstitious? Do you wear amulets or good luck charms? Do you genuinely believe in the horoscope? Have you gone to fortune-tellers, sorcerers, palm-readers, Tarot-card readers, or witches? Have you participated in séances?

2. You shall not invoke the name of the LORD, your God, in vain.

Do you have respect and love for the name of God and of the Virgin Mary? Have you courageously witnessed to your faith? Have you blasphemed? Have you made false or heretical statements about God, for example: "God does not do what is right," "God is cruel," "God is bad," "God enjoys human suffering," "God forgets about good people," etc.? Have you told blasphemous stories or jokes? Have you made oaths falsely, illicitly, or unnecessarily? Have you kept the vows and promises you have made?

3. Remember the sabbath day—keep it holy.

The twenty-four hours of Sunday and feast days constitute "the Lord's Day." Have you made them holy with prayer, good works, the sacred values of life (family, friendship, culture, nature, solidarity, peace, etc.)? Have you freed yourself from the toil of work, enjoying the freedom of the children of God? Have you worked even though you were able to avoid it? Have you participated in the Mass, living one hour together with other believers? At Mass, have you been distracted, have you chatted, have you disturbed others? Have you freely dedicated to others (apart from your relatives) a little of your time, of your capacities? Have you done volunteer work?

4. *Honor your father and your mother.*

Have you loved, respected, obeyed, and listened to your parents according to your abilities? Have you been kind and available in your family? At home, do you participate and share your life with your family? Do you create serenity, communion, conversation with others, or do you make them live in solitude and silence? Are you committed to raising your children? Do you monitor their friendships, games, entertainment, and reading? Do you feel responsible for the school they attend? Do you give them the example of a true Christian life? Do you pray with them as a family? Do you respect your elders, women, children, superiors, the authorities? Do you faithfully obey the laws of the state? Do you do your duty as a good citizen? Do you understand the importance of voting? Have you voted according to your conscience, in keeping with your Christian principles? Have you ever sold your vote to private interests? Do you belong to associations with immoral purposes?

5. *You shall not kill.*

Do you consider your life as a gift from God, of which you are not the absolute master, but an administrator, a user? Do you respect moderation in food, drink, smoking? Do you allow yourself the proper rest? Do you flee from alcoholism and drugs? Have you used drugs? Are you a careful driver?

Have you ever endangered your own life or that of others? Have you taken proper care of your own health and that of your loved ones? Do you try to love others as yourself, and above all as God loves them? Have you done to others what you would like to be done to you? Are you welcoming and supportive, especially with those who have less than you do? Are you envious? Do you cultivate sentiments of hatred, rancor, revenge? Have you quarreled? Do you respect and help the weakest in society: the sick, the handicapped, the elderly, children, the poor? Are you racist? Have you forgiven those who have offended you? Have you had, procured, or recommended an abortion, one of the most serious sins in the eyes of God and of the Church? Have you killed anyone? Have you ever used violence? Have you injured anyone or made anyone ill? Do you own, keep, or use dangerous and offensive weapons? Have you been cruel toward animals? Have you cursed or wished evil upon others? Have you given scandal with your way of dressing, acting, or speaking? Have you been the occasion of sin for someone?

6. *You shall not commit adultery.*

Do you have a Christian conception of love, sexuality, chastity? Have you kept your body pure and chaste? Have you committed dishonest, obscene, immoral acts? Have you given yourself over to lust, to autoeroticism, to prostitution, to sexual perversion, to homosexuality? Have you gone to orgies? Have you had "adventures"? Have you seduced or dishonored any innocent person? Do you avoid bad or dangerous occasions and company? Have you had premarital relations? In marriage, do you have a Christian sense of the sacrament you have received? Do you love, respect, and give generous help to your spouse? Are your marital relations always an expression of love, of total self-giving and fecundity? Have you committed adultery? Have you misused or abused marriage by not observing the law of God and the teaching of the Church? Have you used some form of contraception? Do you read or look at obscene newspapers, magazines, books, programs? Do you consume and enjoy pornographic stories, films, novels? Do you contribute to the development and diffusion of pornography by buying obscene material? At home, do you have any obscene statues or posters, or pornographic images? Do you think or talk about women (or men) as if they were only an object of pleasure? Do you assist and encourage the fidelity of other couples?

7. *You shall not steal.*

Are you convinced of the word of the Gospel according to which "it is impossible for one who is attached to money to enter the kingdom of God"? Do you know that avarice, for the Bible, is "idolatry," meaning the worship of money in the place of God? Are you a usurer? Have you lent money at excessive rates of interest, ruining needy persons already in difficulty? Are you honest at your job, in your profession, at the office, in your business? Have you earned what you own honestly? Have you appropriated the property of the community or of others? Do you believe that you work loyally in such a way that you deserve your monthly salary? Have you wasted time at work? Have you stayed home from work without real necessity? Have you demanded kickbacks, bribes, undue favors? Have you asked for recommendations in order to obtain advantages and privileges? Are you convinced that the dishonesty of others never justifies your own? In addition to your rights, have you also thought about your duties? Do you respect the rights of others? In the claims that you make, even if they are just, do you also take into account the common good? Have you gone on strike without just cause? If you are an employer, do you pay your employees a just wage? Do you defraud the state? Do you pay your taxes honestly? Do you respect what belongs to society: streets, means of transportation, public places, and buildings? Have you harmed the environment, monuments, public or private property, littering or dirtying? Have you repaired or paid for the damage done? Have you given back money or other things taken on a loan? Do you sell yourself to obtain favors or advantages? Have you used illicit means to obtain results at school, at work, in politics, in society? Have you defrauded insurance companies by declaring false damage and obtaining payment unjustly? Have you always met your responsibilities? Have you played games of hazard? Are you dedicated to gambling, harming your family? Have you forged checks? Have you intentionally spent counterfeit money? Have you acquired merchandise presented as stolen?

8. *You shall not bear false witness.*

Are you false, unfaithful, deceitful? Do you deceive your neighbor with your words? Have you told lies? Have you given reckless advice? Have you unjustly accused your neighbor? Do you speak poorly of others? Do you gossip? Have you sworn falsely? In giving testimony, have you made false depositions? Have you taught your children or others to lie by your example? Have you cooperated with the errors of others, taking part in them directly and voluntarily? Have you failed to prevent or denounce the errors of others, when you were obliged to do so? Have you protected those who commit wrongs? Have you concealed crimes by wrongful silence? Have you calumniated? Have you defamed someone by gossiping? Have you repaired any defamation or calumny caused?

9. You shall not covet your neighbor's wife (or husband).

Have you preserved modesty and decency in your life and in your thoughts? Do you have a "clean" mind? Have you looked at women (or men) with concupiscence? Have you intentionally enjoyed impure thoughts or desires? Do you use inappropriate attire or behavior to prompt wrongful desires, restlessness, excitement in others? Do you understand that this is moral violence and a scandal?

10. You shall not covet your neighbor's belongings.

Do you always complain about what you have, saying, "They're so lucky . . ."? Do you love luxury and opulence? Do you despise the evangelical value of poverty? Are you envious of the goods and belongings of others? Do you wish evil upon others, and are you happy when bad things happen to others? How do you live what Christ taught: "Blessed are the poor in spirit"?

C. Other Aids for the Examination of Conscience

To make a good examination of conscience, it can be very helpful to review the observance of these other formulas of Catholic doctrine:

✠ The Two Commandments of charity:

1. You shall love the Lord your God with all your heart, with all your soul, and with all your mind.
2. You shall love your neighbor as yourself.

✠ The golden rule (Mt 7:12):

Do to others whatever you would have them do to you.

✠ The Beatitudes (Mt 5:3-12):

Blessed are the poor in spirit, for theirs is the kingdom of heaven.
Blessed are they who mourn, for they will be comforted.
Blessed are the meek, for they will inherit the land.
Blessed are they who hunger and thirst for righteousness, for they will be satisfied.
Blessed are the merciful, for they will be shown mercy.
Blessed are the clean of heart, for they will see God.
Blessed are the peacemakers, for they will be called children of God.
Blessed are they who are persecuted for the sake of righteousness, for theirs is the kingdom of heaven.

> Blessed are you when they insult you and persecute you and utter every kind of evil against you falsely because of me. Rejoice and be glad, for your reward will be great in heaven.

✠ Some other Scripture passages:

"From within people, from their hearts, come evil thoughts, unchastity, theft, murder, adultery, greed, malice, deceit, licentiousness, envy, blasphemy, arrogance, folly. All these evils come from within and they defile" (Mk 7:21-23).

"Do you not know that the unjust will not inherit the kingdom of God? Do not be deceived; neither fornicators nor idolaters nor adulterers nor boy prostitutes nor sodomites nor thieves nor the greedy nor drunkards nor slanderers nor robbers will inherit the kingdom of God" (1 Cor 6:9-10).

"But as for cowards, the unfaithful, the depraved, murderers, the unchaste, sorcerers, idol-worshipers, and deceivers of every sort, their lot is in the burning pool of fire and sulfur, which is the second death" (Rev 21:8).

✠ The three theological virtues:

1. Faith
2. Hope
3. Charity

✠ The four cardinal virtues:

1. Prudence
2. Justice
3. Fortitude
4. Temperance

✠ The five precepts of the Church:

1. Participate in Mass on Sundays and on the other days commanded and remain free from work and activities that could prevent the sanctification of these days.
2. Go to confession at least once a year.
3. Receive the Sacrament of the Eucharist at least during the Easter season.
4. Abstain from eating meat and observe fasting on the days established by the Church.
5. Contribute to the material needs of the Church as possible.

✠ The seven corporal works of mercy:

1. Feed the hungry.
2. Give drink to the thirsty.
3. Clothe the naked.
4. Give shelter to pilgrims.
5. Visit the sick.
6. Visit the imprisoned.
7. Bury the dead.

✠ The seven spiritual works of mercy:

1. Counsel the doubtful.
2. Instruct the ignorant.
3. Admonish sinners.
4. Console the afflicted.
5. Forgive offenses.
6. Bear wrongs patiently.
7. Pray to God for the living and the dead.

✠ The seven capital vices:

1. Pride
2. Greed
3. Lust
4. Anger
5. Gluttony
6. Envy
7. Sloth

✠ Sins that cry out to heaven for vengeance:

1. Voluntary homicide
2. Sins of impurity against nature
3. Oppression of the poor
4. Defrauding workers of their just wages

For more on this topic:

> *Redazione delle ESD, Sintesi della morale cattolica.* Ed. Studio Domenicano, 1995, pp. 101-108
> *Catechism of the Catholic Church*, Part Three
> *Compendium of the CCC*, Part Three

VIII
What Is Moral Conscience?

It is said: Everyone must act according to conscience . . . do what you think is best . . . follow your conscience . . . This is true. But we often forget to ask ourselves: What sort of conscience? What characteristics should the conscience have? How is the conscience formed?

This section is intended to respond to these and other questions, and wherever conscience is discussed, what is meant is always moral conscience.

We will begin by asking ourselves:

What is the moral conscience?

✠ Present in the deepest part of the person, the conscience is

- "A judgment of reason whereby the human person recognizes the moral quality of a concrete act that he is going to perform, is in the process of performing, or has already completed" (CCC, no. 1778). Without the use of reason, conscience does not exist.

- The natural perception of the fundamental moral principles, their application in particular circumstances, and the final judgment on what one is to do (or has done)
- "The most secret core and sanctuary of a man" (*Gaudium et Spes*, no. 16)
- The sanctuary of the person, which decides on his or her actions

✠ It is not, however

- An immediate opinion, which is so often instead the result of a particular state of mind or outside pressure, for example by the media or majority opinion
- Connected to instinct or to relativistic subjectivism, which leads to affirming that there can be no authority higher than the conscience
- The source of truth and values
- An absolute, placed above truth and error, good and evil
- A manner of acting according to one's personal interpretation or whim without answering to anyone

What is the task of conscience?

✠ It allows us to

- Perceive the principles of morality
- Apply them to actual events and circumstances through a practical discernment of motivations and purposes

- Do good and avoid evil
- Express judgments on the moral quality of concrete actions that are to be performed or have already been performed
- Take responsibility for what we have done

"If man commits evil, the just judgment of conscience can remain within him as the witness to the universal truth of the good, at the same time as the evil of his particular choice. The verdict of the judgment of conscience remains a pledge of hope and mercy. In attesting to the fault committed, it calls to mind the forgiveness that must be asked, the good that must still be practiced, and the virtue that must be constantly cultivated with the grace of God" (CCC, no. 1781).

✠ Conscience therefore has a threefold task:

- *Deductive*: It knows, recognizes, and applies moral norms to various situations and decisions.
- *Imperative*: It decides the moral behavior of the person in the light of the moral law, of the inner voice of the Spirit, of the teachings of Christ transmitted in a certain and authoritative manner on the part of the pastors chosen by Christ himself.
- *Creative*: It adopts strategies, plans solutions, and identifies tonalities and modalities for doing good.

✠ "[Conscience] bears witness to the authority of truth in reference to the supreme Good to which the human person is drawn, and it welcomes the commandments" (CCC, no. 1777). It is therefore necessary to affirm the *primacy of the truth* rather than the primacy of the conscience. The conscience is the seat of our decisions, it is the place where we decide, but it is not the criterion of the decision. We do not establish the criterion on our own: it is given to us by God, who is Love, who is Truth.

What is the indispensable condition for hearing the voice of conscience?

"It is important for every person to be sufficiently present to himself in order to hear and follow the voice of his conscience. This requirement of interiority is all the more necessary as life often distracts us from any reflection, self-examination or introspection. 'Return to your conscience, question it. . . . Turn inward, brethren, and in everything you do, see God as your witness'" (CCC, no. 1779).

What must the conscience be like?

It must be

- True
- Certain
- Upright
- Free
- Formed

When is the conscience true?

✠ A conscience is true when it is founded on the truth. In fact, the conscience is an act of reason aimed at the truth of things.

"The moral conscience, to be able to judge human conduct rightly, above all must be based on the solid foundation of truth, that is, it must be enlightened to know the true value of actions and the solid criteria for evaluation. Therefore, it must be able to distinguish good from evil, even where the social environment, pluralistic culture and superimposed interests do not help it do so" (Pope Benedict XVI, Address, February 24, 2007).

"For man has in his heart a law written by God. To obey it is the very dignity of man; according to it he will be judged . . . In a wonderful manner conscience reveals that law which is fulfilled by love of God and neighbor" (*Gaudium et Spes*, no. 16).

It is therefore necessary to proclaim, defend, and promote the possibility for reason to

- Know the truth. Today there is even mistrust of the capacity of reason to perceive the truth. Just as it also happens that the reduction of knowledge to subjective certainty leads at the same time to the renunciation of the truth.
- Not interpret this reality as it appears to and pleases each one. Conscience is an antidote to, rather than an excuse for, subjectivism (according to which that which one thinks is the criterion and source of truth)

and relativism (according to which the truth does not exist, but instead there are many truths).
- Recognize the *splendor* of the truth, its transcendence with regard to our created intelligence, and as a result, our duty to be open to it, to accept it not as our own invention, but as a gift that comes from God

Why is it important that the conscience be certain?

Because the person must always act, in the moral sphere, in all certainty and security, in order to be always fully responsible for his or her actions. When making a decision, the person must do so with a certain conscience, and this means that the conscience must be sure, it must issue its moral judgment with certainty, and not be in doubt, not knowing what is the right thing to do. In such a case, he or she must first consult trusted and competent persons in order to resolve all doubt and act in the certainty acquired.

What does it mean that the conscience must be upright?

It means that the conscience must "be in accord with what is just and good according to reason and the law of God" (*Compendium of the* CCC, no. 373). It is the very dignity of the human person that implies and demands this rectitude. The upright conscience is therefore determined to follow the truth without contradictions, without betrayals, and without compromises.

Can the conscience also issue an erroneous judgment?

✠ The conscience is not always right, it is not infallible. If it were, there would be no single truth, because often the judgments of conscience are in contradiction, among different persons and even within the same person. There would be as many truths as there are consciences; there would be only the truth of the individual person, and therefore as many truths as there are persons.

✠ The conscience can issue an erroneous judgment, which happens when its judgment departs from reason and the divine law.

"A person must always obey the certain judgment of his own conscience but he could make erroneous judgments for reasons that may not always exempt him from personal guilt. However, an evil act committed through involuntary ignorance is not imputable to the person, even though the act remains objectively evil. One must therefore work to correct the errors of moral conscience" (*Compendium of the CCC*, no. 376).

✠ Nevertheless, the erroneous conscience does not lose its dignity.

When is ignorance culpable?

✠ This is so in the case of "a man who cares but little for truth and goodness, or of a conscience which by degrees grows practically sightless as a result of habitual sin" (*Gaudium et Spes*, no. 16). In these cases, the person is culpable for the evil that he or she commits.

✠ "Ignorance of Christ and his Gospel, bad example given by others, enslavement to one's passions, assertion of a mistaken notion of autonomy of conscience, rejection of the Church's authority and her teaching, lack of conversion and of charity: these can be at the source of errors of judgment in moral conduct" (CCC, no. 1792).

When is ignorance involuntary and invincible (and therefore non-culpable)?

✠ When the ignorance cannot be attributed to the responsibility of the person. Nevertheless, in this case, even though the person is not subjectively responsible for the evil committed, the evil committed remains an evil, an objective disorder. The fact that the blind do not see the sun does not allow one to conclude that the sun does not exist.

✠ This leads to the responsibility of the person to

- Become informed about the evil
- Correct his or her moral conscience of its errors
- Repair as much as possible the harm done by the evil committed

Is the erroneous conscience always justified?

✠ The erroneous conscience cannot be justified if its being in error is due to culpable ignorance or to an obfuscation of the conscience.

Ignorance cannot be considered a convenient solution, an advantage. This would be like saying that not knowing is better than knowing.

"No longer seeing offenses, the silencing of the voice of conscience in so many areas of life is a spiritual disease much more dangerous than the offense that one is still able to recognize as such. Those who are no longer able to recognize that killing is a sin have fallen more deeply than those who can still recognize the evil of their behavior, because they have drawn further away from the truth than from conversion" (Cardinal Joseph Ratzinger, "In Praise of Conscience," Conference of March 16, 1991).

✠ One of the Psalms contains this statement, which is always worthy of consideration: "Who can detect trespasses? Cleanse me from my inadvertent sins" (Ps 19:13).

✠ It can therefore happen that the offense is found not in the act of the moment, not in the immediate judgment of my conscience, but is found elsewhere, deeper: in the carelessness and closure that I have cultivated, albeit gradually, toward life.

When is the conscience free?

✠ The person has the right to act in full freedom according to his or her conscience. This freedom means that he or she

- Cannot be forced to act against his or her conscience (see Rom 14:23): "In all he says and does, man is

obliged to follow faithfully what he knows to be just and right" (CCC, no. 1778).
- Can neither be prevented from acting according to his or her conscience, above all in the area of religion

✠ This freedom is limited, however. One must follow one's conscience

- Without going against the common good
- In respect for those values that are non-negotiable, precisely because they correspond to objective truths, universal and equal for all

What norms must the conscience always follow?

"There are three general norms:

- One may never do evil so that good may result from it.
- The so-called Golden Rule, 'Whatever you wish that men would do to you, do so to them' (Mt 7:12).
- Charity always proceeds by way of respect for one's neighbor and his conscience, even though this does not mean accepting as good something that is objectively evil" (*Compendium of the CCC*, no. 375).

When is a conscience well-formed?

✠ A conscience is well-formed when it is certain, upright, and truthful, which means that it "formulates its judgments according to reason, in conformity with the true good willed by the wisdom of the Creator" (CCC, no. 1783).

✠ The more informed and formed a conscience is, the more free it is.

✠ The conscience, like a spring of water, can also be polluted, deviated, adulterated. But in this case, it can also be helped to purify itself, to return to the right path, through adequate information and formation, always in respect of its freedom and dignity.

✠ A well-formed conscience presents itself as an authentic exercise of wise discernment, of free and responsible decisions. The reduction of conscience to subjective certainty does not liberate, but enslaves, making us totally dependent on personal taste or prevailing opinion.

Is it necessary to form the conscience?

Forming, educating the conscience is "indispensable for human beings who are subjected to negative influences and tempted by sin to prefer their own judgment and to reject authoritative teachings . . . Man is sometimes confronted by situations that make moral judgments less assured and decision difficult. But he must always seriously seek what is right and good and discern the will of God expressed in divine law" (CCC, nos. 1783, 1787).

Education helps the conscience to refine itself, albeit gradually, like a high-precision instrument. Education must serve above all to lead the conscience to know, embrace, and follow the truth. Let us not fall into the error of thinking that remaining far from the truth would be better for us than the truth, almost as if being in the darkness were better than being in the light!

"A man of conscience is one who never buys, at the price of renouncing the truth, getting along, prosperity, success, social consideration and approval on the part of dominant opinion . . . the identification of the conscience with superficial understanding, the reduction of man to his subjectivity does not at all liberate, but enslaves; it makes us totally dependent on the dominant opinions and also lowers the level of these day after day" ("In Praise of Conscience").

How long does the education of a conscience last?

✠ "The education of the conscience is a lifelong task. From the earliest years, it awakens the child to the knowledge and practice of the interior law recognized by conscience. Prudent education teaches virtue; it prevents or cures fear, selfishness and pride, resentment arising from guilt, and feelings of complacency, born of human weakness and faults. The education of the conscience guarantees freedom and engenders peace of heart" (CCC, no. 1784).

✠ "One must be re-educated to the desire to know authentic truth, to defend one's own freedom of choice in regard to mass behavior and the lures of propaganda, to nourish passion for moral beauty and a clear conscience. This is the delicate duty of parents and educators who assist them; and it is the duty of the Christian community with regard to its faithful. Concerning the Christian conscience, its growth and nourishment, one cannot be content with fleeting contact with the principal truths of faith in infancy, but a program of accompaniment is necessary along the various stages of life, opening the mind and the heart to welcome the fundamental duties upon which the existence of the individual and the community rest" (Pope Benedict XVI, Address, February 24, 2007).

✠ It should not be forgotten what St. Augustine wrote: "You have made us for yourself, O Lord, and our hearts are restless until they rest in you" (*Confessions*, I, 1).

How is the conscience formed so that it is upright and truthful?

✠ "An upright and true moral conscience is formed by education and by assimilating the Word of God and the teaching of the Church. It is supported by the gifts of the Holy Spirit and helped by the advice of wise people. Prayer and an examination of conscience can also greatly assist one's moral formation" (*Compendium of the CCC*, no. 374).

✠ It is also important to interpret experiences and the signs of the times with the virtue of prudence, which "is the virtue that disposes practical reason to discern our true good in every circumstance and to choose the right means of achieving it" (CCC, no. 1806).

✠ In this way, the prudent person, through his or her conscience

- Hears the voice of God

- Perceives and recognizes the precepts of the divine law
- Applies moral principles to individual cases without error and overcomes doubts about the good to be done and the evil to be avoided

✠ Allowing one's conscience to be illuminated by the Christian faith allows one to

- Know the truth and live one's life in authentic and full happiness. The faith, in fact, is not a weight, a heavy burden, something that brings sadness, an imposition of moral demands. The way that leads to truth and goodness is not a comfortable way, but a high and arduous way. On this way, however, we are not alone: Christ is with us, he gives us the Holy Spirit who is the Spirit of truth and happiness.
- Overcome objectivism and relativism. "One cannot identify the conscience of man with the self-awareness of the ego, with objective certainty about oneself and one's moral behavior. On the one hand, this awareness can be a mere reflection of the social environment and of the opinions present in it. On the other hand, it can stem from a lack of self-criticism, from an inability to listen to the depths of one's own spirit" ("In Praise of Conscience").

✠ Here is the importance of the Magisterium in this regard.

What is the role of the Magisterium of the Church in the formation of the conscience?

✠ I have said that the judgment of one's own conscience must be illuminated by the truth, and, to this end, especially with problems that are new or that present themselves in completely unprecedented terms, recourse to the Magisterium is of great help for the formation of a certain, true, upright conscience.

✠ In fact, the Magisterium of the Church is not

- An obstacle, but a help, given by Christ to all people of good will in seeking, finding, and welcoming the truth. It exists so that the moral conscience may safely reach the truth and remain in it.
- Just any sort of external source of moral thought with which the individual conscience must come into contact. It informs the conscience practically as the soul informs the body.
- A reality that restricts, threatens, or even denies the freedom of the personal conscience, but rather an aid for the illumination of the conscience

✠ It cannot be forgotten that the Magisterium of the Church (meaning the pope in communion with the bishops) was willed by Christ himself, who entrusted to it the mission of serving the Word of God, "teaching only what has been handed on, listening to it devoutly, guarding it scrupulously, and explaining it faithfully by divine commission and with the help of the Holy Spirit; it draws from this one deposit of faith everything which it presents for belief as divinely revealed" (*Dei Verbum*, no. 10).

Therefore, "mindful of Christ's words to his apostles: 'He who hears you, hears me,' the faithful receive with docility the teachings and directives that their pastors give them in different forms" (CCC, no. 87).

✠ The Magisterium therefore seeks to help consciences to reach a more reliable mediation and application of moral truth. It is always the objective moral truth that has the primacy, and only this can be infallibly true.

What is the role of the Holy Spirit in the formation of the conscience?

The conscience is like a space inhabited by the Holy Spirit, who frees us not from the outside, but in the depths of our heart, configuring us to Christ so that we may decide and act as he did.

The Holy Spirit has been given to us in Baptism by God the Father, through Jesus Christ dead and risen, "until we all attain to the unity of faith and knowledge of the Son of God, to mature manhood, to the extent of the full stature of Christ" (Eph 4:13).

What is conscientious objection?

✠ "The citizen is obliged in conscience not to follow the directives of civil authorities when they are contrary to the demands of the moral order, to the fundamental rights of persons or the teachings of the Gospel. Refusing obedience to civil authorities, when their demands are contrary to those of an upright conscience, finds its justification in the distinction between serving God and serving the political community. 'Repay therefore to Caesar the things that are Caesar's, and to God the things that are God's' (Mt 22:21). 'We must obey God rather than men'" (CCC, no. 2242).

✠ Courageous conscientious objection must be promoted and supported, since more and more laws are being established in society that are contrary to nonnegotiable principles and values, like

- Respect for human life, its defense from conception to natural death
- The family built upon marriage between a man and a woman
- The freedom to educate one's children and the promotion of the common good in all its forms (*Sacramentum Caritatis*, no. 83)

✠ The state must recognize in its legislation the right to conscientious objection every time that a citizen believes it is necessary to resort to it, above all in the field of medical ethics. Unfortunately, there exists in the current context a paradox, according to which a society that is ideologically tolerant (in the contemporary sense of the term) often is not, however, willing to tolerate conscientious objection, because such a society does not accept that

- There can be anyone who to any extent escapes its control, the observance of its laws, or opposes its ideological and social totalitarianism

- There can be fundamental values that transcend the civil laws themselves, which in this case would no longer have an absolute value that is binding for all

✠ Conscientious objection, if it is accompanied by a love for the truth that is extended to each person

- Is an exemplary act that has the courage of consistency
- Is not a shirking of responsibility, but on the contrary, the acceptance of bearing witness
- Extends to a very complex and vast set of circumstances (it should be enough to think only of the category of physicians active today in the ample field of human life—abortion, euthanasia, abortifacient pills, the use of embryos in research . . .)
- Is a final means (a human right and duty) to avoid being involved in actions that a person finds deeply repugnant
- Is an expression and implementation of the legitimate right to freedom that every person has, by virtue of which one can and must refuse to commit an action that is opposed to or violates the principles—ethical and/or religious—that his or her conscience dictates

For more on this topic:

Catechism of the Catholic Church, nos. 1776-1802
Compendium of the CCC, nos. 372-376

IX
Priesthood

Who is the priest?

He is the one who has received the Sacrament of Holy Orders from the hands of a validly consecrated bishop.

What is the Sacrament of Holy Orders?

It is one of the Seven Sacraments instituted by Christ, through which is given, to the one who receives it, "a special consecration (ordination). Through a special gift of the Holy Spirit, this sacrament enables the ordained to exercise a sacred power in the name and with the authority of Christ for the service of the People of God" (*Compendium of the CCC*, no. 323).

What are the effects of the Sacrament of Holy Orders?

"This sacrament yields a special outpouring of the Holy Spirit which configures the recipient to Christ in his triple office as Priest, Prophet, and King, according to the respective degrees of the sacrament. Ordination confers an indelible spiritual character and therefore cannot be repeated or conferred for a limited time" (*Compendium of the CCC*, no. 335).

With what authority is the priestly ministry exercised?

"Ordained priests in the exercise of their sacred ministry speak and act not on their own authority, nor even by mandate or delegation of the community, but rather in the Person of Christ the Head and in the name of the Church. Therefore, the ministerial priesthood differs essentially and not just in degree from the priesthood common to all the faithful for whose service Christ instituted it" (*Compendium of the CCC*, no. 336).

Why is the priest necessary?

Because this is what Christ wanted in instituting his Church. The will of Christ is therefore the fundamental and decisive factor. It is Christ himself who willed that, without the priest, there cannot be the celebration of two essential sacraments: Eucharist and Penance.

"The sacramental character which distinguishes them by virtue of their reception of Holy Orders ensures that their presence and ministry are unique, indispensable and irreplaceable" (Pope John Paul II, *Letter to Priests*, Holy Thursday 2000).

What is the mission of the priest?

✠ His mission is unique:

- He acts in the name and in the person of Christ the head (*in persona Christi capitis*) for the good of souls. "Only Christ is the true priest, the others are his ministers" (St. Thomas Aquinas, *Commentary on the Letter to the Hebrews*, c. 7, lect. 4).
- He is a collaborator of the bishop in a particular church. He receives "from the bishop the charge of a parish community or a determinate ecclesial office" (CCC, no. 1595).
- He forms together with the other presbyters a "single diocesan presbytery," in communion with and under the authority of the bishop, to whom he owes obedience (see *Presbyterorum Ordinis*, no. 8).
- He is consecrated to
  - Preach the Gospel
  - To celebrate divine worship, especially the Eucharist from which his ministry draws its strength
  - And to be a shepherd of the faithful (*Compendium of the CCC*, no. 328)

✠ "Through the sacrament of Holy Orders priests share in the universal dimensions of the mission that Christ entrusted to the apostles. The spiritual gift they have received in ordination prepares them, not for a limited and restricted mission, 'but for the fullest, in fact the universal mission of salvation "to the end of the earth,'" 'prepared in spirit to preach the Gospel everywhere'" (CCC, no. 1565).

What are the characteristics of the priest's mission?

His mission is

- "Ecclesial," because no one proclaims himself in the first person, but within and through his own humanity every priest must be well aware that he is bringing to the world Another, God himself. God is the only treasure that, ultimately, people desire to find in a priest.
- "Communional," because it is carried out in a unity and communion that only secondly has also important aspects of social visibility. Moreover, these derive essentially from that divine intimacy in which the priest is called to be expert, so that he may be able to lead the souls entrusted to him humbly and trustingly to the same encounter with the Lord.
- "Hierarchical" and "doctrinal." These dimensions suggest reaffirming the importance of the ecclesiastical discipline (the term has a connection with "disciple") and doctrinal training and not only theological, initial and continuing formation (Pope Benedict XVI, Address to the members of the Congregation for the Clergy on the occasion of their plenary assembly, March 16, 2009).

What does the priest's special bond with Christ entail?

✠ The priest is intimately united with Christ to such an extent as to be and to act "in the name of Christ," the supreme and eternal Priest, by virtue of the anointing of the Holy Spirit.

✠ This means and entails

- His being a priest is not his own achievement, nor does it come from an *election* of a community or group, but it is the fruit of the gratuitous call of God: "It was not you who chose me, but I who chose you and appointed you to go and bear fruit that will remain" (Jn 15:16). This call is recognized and welcomed in freedom on the part of the individual, and is confirmed and authenticated by the ordaining bishop.
- The priest is marked by a special indelible spiritual *character*, which conforms him to Christ as priest, prophet, and king. In this way he participates in "the authority by which Christ Himself builds up, sanctifies, and rules His Body" (*Presbyterorum Ordinis*, no. 2).
- His action is a true service. "It is entirely related to Christ and to men. It depends entirely on Christ and on his unique priesthood; it has been instituted for the good of men and the communion of the Church. The sacrament of Holy Orders communicates a 'sacred power' which is none other than that of Christ. The exercise of this authority must therefore be measured against the model of Christ, who by love made himself the least and the servant of all" (CCC, no. 1551).
- The mission received by the priest is to be exercised not at his pleasure, but *in the name of Christ*, of whom he is a minister and sign, as shown above all by the

testimony of Christ, ever more in keeping with that of Christ. He is the repeater, the spokesman of the Word of an Other: Christ. "Receive the Gospel of Christ, whose herald you have become. Believe what you read, teach what you believe, practice what you teach" (Rite of Ordination).

- "Not wanting to impose our own way and our own will, not desiring to become someone else, but abandoning ourselves to him, however and wherever he wants to use us" (Pope Benedict XVI, Homily, Holy Thursday 2009)
- "It is Christ himself who acts in those whom he chooses as his ministers; he supports them so that their response develops in a dimension of trust and gratitude that removes all fear, even when they experience more acutely their own weakness (cf. Rom 8:26-28), or indeed when the experience of misunderstanding or even of persecution is most bitter (cf. Rom 8:35-39)" (Pope Benedict XVI, Message for the 46th World Day of Prayer for Vocations, January 20, 2009)

☧ Even wearing the liturgical vestments, in particular when celebrating the Eucharist, indicates visibly that the priest is and acts "in the name of Christ." In this external sign, the liturgical garment makes "the interior event visible to us, as well as our task which stems from it: putting on Christ; giving ourselves to him as he gave himself to us . . . The fact that we are standing at the altar clad in liturgical vestments must make it clearly visible to those present that we are there 'in the person of an Other'" (Pope Benedict XVI, Homily, Holy Thursday 2007).

In what sense does the priest act "in the name of the whole Church"?

✠ "The ministerial priesthood has the task not only of representing Christ—Head of the Church—before the assembly of the faithful, but also of acting in the name of the whole Church when presenting to God the prayer of the Church, and above all when offering the Eucharistic sacrifice.

✠ "'In the name of the *whole* Church' does not mean that priests are the delegates of the community. The prayer and offering of the Church are inseparable from the prayer and offering of Christ, her head; it is always the case that Christ worships in and through his Church. The whole Church, the Body of Christ, prays and offers herself 'through him, with him, in him,' in the unity of the Holy Spirit, to God the Father. The whole Body, *caput et membra*, prays and offers itself, and therefore those who in the Body are especially his ministers are called ministers not only of Christ, but also of the Church. It is because the ministerial priesthood represents Christ that it can represent the Church" (CCC, nos. 1552-1553).

What do people expect from the priest?

"The faithful expect only one thing from priests: that they be specialists in promoting the encounter between man and God. The priest is not asked to be an expert in economics, construction or politics. He is expected to be an expert in the spiritual life . . . What the faithful expect from him is that he be a witness to the eternal wisdom contained in the revealed word" (Pope Benedict XVI, Address to clergy, Warsaw Cathedral, May 25, 2006).

This is why it is more important than ever to ensure the suitability of candidates for the priesthood, and guarantee an adequate and comprehensive priestly formation for those who are studying for the sacred ministry.

Who can become a priest?

✠ Only a baptized male can become one. "The Church recognizes herself to be bound by this choice made by the Lord himself. For this reason the ordination of women is not possible" (CCC, no. 1577).

✠ "No one has a *right* to receive the sacrament of Holy Orders. Indeed no one claims this office for himself; he is called to it by God. Anyone who thinks he recognizes the signs of God's call to the ordained ministry must humbly submit his desire to the authority of the Church, who has the responsibility and right to call someone to receive orders. Like every grace this sacrament can be *received* only as an unmerited gift" (CCC, no. 1578).

✠ Celibacy is required for priests in the Latin Church (see the section "Clerical Celibacy").

✠ "Ask the master of the harvest to send out laborers for his harvest" (Mt 9:38). "Our first duty, therefore, is to keep alive in families and in parishes, in movements and in apostolic associations, in religious communities and in all the sectors of diocesan life this appeal to the divine initiative with unceasing prayer" (Message for the 46th World Day of Prayer for Vocations).

For more on this topic:

Catechism of the Catholic Church, nos. 1562-1592
Compendium of the CCC, nos. 328-336

X
Clerical Celibacy

Is priestly celibacy a dogma of the Church?

✠ The obligation of celibacy for priests is not a dogma, but a disciplinary law of the Church. Nevertheless, this law is very ancient, based on firmly established tradition and on strong motivations.

✠ Virginity is certainly not required by the nature of the priesthood itself. The proof is that celibacy applies for the Latin Church, but not for the Eastern rites, where, even in the communities united with the Catholic Church, married priests are the norm. However, they must be married before they are ordained priests.

✠ Nonetheless, in the Eastern Churches celibacy is required for bishops, as well as for monks. It is also permitted that men already married may be ordained priests. If he is widowed, the priest cannot remarry.

✠ The Church is firmly convinced that the law of sacred celibacy must continue to accompany the ecclesiastical ministry of Latin priests today. It thus maintains that the way of self-donation in celibacy is the normative one for the Latin priestly ministry. Celibacy, although not required by "the very nature of the priesthood . . . accords with the priesthood on many scores" (*Presbyterorum Ordinis*, no. 16).

✠ Moreover, it must not be forgotten that young men who request and freely accept to be consecrated priests in the Latin Church know very well that they must commit themselves to celibacy as well, and make this commitment freely and solemnly before God and the Church.

When was celibacy introduced in the Church?

✠ Among the Apostles, chosen by Christ himself, some were married and others were not, for example the Apostle John.

✠ The obligation of priestly celibacy has been in effect since the fourth century. But at the same time, it must be emphasized that the legislators in the fourth century maintained that this ecclesiastical law was founded on an Apostolic Tradition. For example, the Council of Carthage (AD 390) said: "It is fitting that those who serve the divine mysteries should be perfectly continent (*continentes esse in omnibus*), so that we as well may observe that which the apostles taught and the ancient Church observed."

✠ Afterward, the Magisterium of the Church, through councils and documents, has always reiterated the dispositions on ecclesiastical celibacy. The ecumenical council Vatican II itself reaffirmed, in the declaration *Presbyterorum Ordinis* (no. 16), the close connection between celibacy and the Kingdom of God, seeing the former as a sign that proclaims the latter in a radiant manner.

In what Gospel passages is celibacy discussed?

It is spoken of in Mark 10:29, Matthew 19:12 ("eunuchs for the kingdom of heaven"), and Luke 18:28-30. "Then Peter said, 'We have given up our possessions and followed you.' He said to them, 'Amen, I say to you, there is no one who has given up house or wife or brothers or parents or children for the sake of the kingdom of God who will not receive [back] an overabundant return in this present age and eternal life in the age to come'" (Lk 18:28-30).

In what sense is celibacy a gift?

✠ It is above all an inestimable gift from God, "a special gift of God by which sacred ministers can adhere more easily to Christ with an undivided heart and are able to dedicate themselves more freely to the service of God and humanity" (CIC, c. 277 §1). In this sense, it presupposes a particular vocation, a special call on the part of God, and is therefore a charism.

✠ It is also a special gift of the person to God and neighbor. The radical love of the celibate priest for God is manifested and realized in generous love for his brothers and sisters, in his openness to serve them.

✠ This gift, if it is welcomed and lived with love, joy, and gratitude, is a source of happiness and holiness for the priest himself and for the whole Church.

What are the reasons in favor of celibacy?

✠ It must be stated immediately that exclusively pragmatic and functional reasons, for example reference to greater availability, are not enough. Even more unacceptable are reasons connected in some way to prestige, power, social advancement, or financial benefits, or to an attitude of rejection, fear, or disdain toward marriage.

✠ At the same time, it must be remembered that, as Christ himself said of celibacy and its authentic motivations, "Not all can accept [this] word, but only those to whom that is granted" (Mt 19:11).

✠ There are three real and profound reasons: theocentric-Christological, ecclesiological, and eschatological. These establish the profound suitability that exists between the priesthood and celibacy.

1. The Theocentric-Christological Reason

✠ Celibacy is based on faith in God and on the love of God and for God: it is accepting God like the land on which to found one's existence. The words of the Holy Father Benedict XVI are enlightening in this regard: "The true foundation of celibacy can be contained in the phrase: *Dominus pars*—You are my land. It can only be theocentric. It cannot mean being deprived of love, but must mean letting oneself be consumed by passion for God and subsequently, thanks to a more intimate way of being with him, to serve men and women, too. Celibacy must be a witness to faith: faith in God materializes in that form of life which only has meaning if it is based on God. Basing one's life on him, renouncing marriage and the family, means that I accept and experience God as a reality and that I can therefore bring him to men and women" (Pope Benedict XVI, Address to the members of the Roman curia at the traditional exchange of Christmas greetings, December 22, 2006).

✠ The priest is therefore not a person devoid of love. On the contrary, he lives on passion for God. His life is not that of a bachelor, but of someone indissolubly married to God and his Church. Celibacy is a life for love and of love; it fosters a special kind of spousal love on the part of the priest. The priest is a man of God because he lives for him, speaks of him, discerns and decides with him, is ever more in love with him. A deterioration in the spiritual life very often precedes a crisis of celibacy.

✠ But God has made himself visible and present in Jesus, the only-begotten Son of the Father sent into the world: "He became man, in order that humanity which was subject to sin and death might be reborn, and through this new birth might enter the kingdom of heaven. Being entirely consecrated to the will of the Father, Jesus brought forth this new creation by means of His Paschal mystery" (Pope Paul VI, *Sacerdotalis Caelibatus*, no. 19). Jesus Christ is therefore the newness of God. He renews all things. One important aspect of this newness is life in virginity, which Jesus himself lived. In fact, he remained in the state of virginity his whole life, dedicating himself completely to the service of God and of humanity. Celibacy therefore allows complete dedication to the Lord; a fuller configuration to the Lord Jesus Christ, Head and Bridegroom of the Church; an imitation of his state of life; an identification with the heart of Christ the Bridegroom who gives his life for his Bride; and a greater openness to listening to his Word and to dialogue with him in prayer.

The encyclical *Sacerdotalis Caelibatus* further explains, "Christ remained throughout His whole life in the state of celibacy, which signified His total dedication to the service of God and men. This deep concern between celibacy and the priesthood of Christ is reflected in those whose fortune it is to share in the dignity and mission of the Mediator and eternal Priest; this sharing will be more perfect the freer the sacred minister is from the bonds of flesh and blood" (no. 21).

Virginity for the Kingdom of God therefore exists in the Church because Christ exists, who makes it possible with the gift of his Spirit. "In this bond between the Lord Jesus and the priest, an ontological and psychological bond, a sacramental and moral bond, is the foundation and likewise the power for that 'life according to the Spirit' and that 'radicalism of the Gospel' to which every priest is called today and which is fostered by ongoing formation in its spiritual aspect" (Pope John Paul II, *Pastores Dabo Vobis*, no. 72).

✠ On June 10, 2010, at the vigil of the conclusion of the Year for Priests, Benedict XVI said that celibacy is an anticipation of "the world of the resurrection." It is a sign "that God exists, that God enters into my life, and that I can found my life on Christ, on the future life." Therefore celibacy "is a great scandal," not only for the world of today "in which God does not enter," but for Christianity itself, which "does not think anymore of the future of God. The present of this world alone seems sufficient" (Vigil on the occasion of the international meeting of priests, section "Europe").

2. Ecclesiological Reason

✠ Like Christ and in Christ, the priest is united to the Church with an exclusive love, marrying it in a mystical sense. "The consecrated celibacy of the sacred ministers actually manifests the virginal love of Christ for the Church, and the virginal and supernatural fecundity of this marriage" (*Sacerdotalis Caelibatus*, no. 26). The nuptial character of ecclesiastical celibacy expresses and embodies precisely this relationship between Christ and the Church.

✠ By virtue of this exclusive spousal bond, the celibate priest dedicates himself completely to the generous and disinterested service of Christ and his Church, with great spiritual freedom and on behalf of all, without distinction or discrimination.

In *Presbyterorum Ordinis* we read that priests "dedicate themselves more freely in him and through him to the service of God and men, and they more expeditiously minister to his Kingdom and the work of heavenly regeneration, and thus they are apt to accept, in a broad sense, paternity in Christ" (no. 16).

✠ Ordinary experience teaches and confirms that it is easier for those not bound by other ties of affection to open their hearts to their brothers and sisters completely and without reservation.

3. The Eschatological Reason

Priestly celibacy is a sign and prophecy of the new creation, of the definitive Kingdom of God in the Parousia, when, at the end of this world, all of us will rise from the dead. Virginity lived out of love for the Kingdom of God constitutes a special sign of these last times, because the Lord has proclaimed that "at the resurrection they neither marry nor are given in marriage but are like the angels in heaven" (Mt 22:30).

The future Kingdom is already present in the Church. The Church does not only proclaim it, but realizes it sacramentally by contributing to the "new creation." The Church constitutes the seed and beginning of this Kingdom here below, as the Second Vatican Council teaches (see *Lumen Gentium*, no. 5). Priestly celibacy is one of the ways in which the Church proclaims and contributes to realizing this newness of the Kingdom of God.

Would the abolition of celibacy increase the number of priests?

As the synod of bishops also affirmed in 2005, a relaxation of the rule of celibacy would not be a solution for the problem of the scarcity of vocations, as demonstrated by the experience of the other Christian denominations that have married priests or pastors. The numeric scarcity of priests is to be attributed to other causes, starting with secularized modern culture.

What is the relationship between priestly celibacy and the Sacrament of Matrimony?

It is a complementary relationship: each of them completes the other.

✠ Here are three authoritative testimonies in this regard:

1. "The Risen Lord's spousal love for his Church, offered in the sacrament of marriage, also raises up in the church the gift of virginity for the kingdom. In its turn, virginity indicates the final destiny of conjugal love" (Pope John Paul II, Address to the members of the John Paul II Institute for Studies on Marriage and Family, May 31, 2001).

2. "The choice of virginity for the love of God and the brethren, which is required for priesthood and for consecrated life, goes hand in hand with the estimation of Christian marriage: both, in two different and complementary ways, make visible in a certain way the mystery of God's Covenant with his people"

(Pope Benedict XVI, Address to the participants in the Ecclesial Diocesan Convention of Rome, June 6, 2005).

3. "Both the sacrament of Matrimony and virginity for the Kingdom of God come from the Lord himself. It is he who gives them meaning and grants them the grace which is indispensable for living them out in conformity with his will. Esteem of virginity for the sake of the kingdom and the Christian understanding of marriage are inseparable, and they reinforce each other" (CCC, no. 1620).

✠ The celibate person makes married persons aware of the fact that they do not exist solely as a function of their relationship but have their own value. And married persons bear witness for the celibate person to the necessity of giving one's life a dimension of embodied love.

Is the priest a man alone?

"By reason of his celibacy the priest is a man alone: that is true, but his solitude is not meaningless emptiness because it is filled with God and the brimming riches of His kingdom. Moreover, he has prepared himself for this solitude—which should be an internal and external plenitude of charity—if he has chosen it with full understanding, and not through any proud desire to be different from the rest of men, or to withdraw himself from common responsibilities, or to alienate himself from his brothers, or to show contempt for the world. Though set apart from the world, the priest is not separated from the People of God, because he has been 'appointed to act on behalf of men,' since he is 'consecrated' completely to charity and to the work for which the Lord has chosen him. At times loneliness will weigh heavily on the priest, but he will not for that reason regret having generously chosen it. Christ, too, in the most tragic hours of His life was alone" (*Sacerdotalis Caelibatus*, nos. 58-59).

What does the priest require in order to remain celibate?

✠ He requires

- Careful preparation during his journey toward this objective, and therefore an adequate formation
  - Within his family
  - Above all during his years at the seminary
- A solid human and Christian formation, supported by good spiritual direction, both as a seminarian and as a priest
- A deeper and deeper experience of Christ. The quality and depth of this relationship with the Lord will determine his entire existence as a priest.
- An ever more comprehensive and radical sharing in the sentiments and attitudes of Jesus Christ
- Constant prayer that ceaselessly calls upon God as the living God and trusts in him in times of confusion just as in times of joy. The daily celebration of the Eucharist, the Divine Office, frequent confession, adoration of the Most Holy Sacrament, an affectionate relationship with Mary Most Holy, retreats, daily

recitation of the Holy Rosary if possible . . . these are some of the forms of prayer that must never be lacking in the priestly life.

- A willingness to follow Christ on the way of Calvary as well. The priestly life also involves the acceptance of the perspective of the Crucified One. Suffering, fatigue, discomfort, disappointment, boredom, even defeat have their place in the life of the priest, who nonetheless is able to and must react to all of this with God's help.

- "A particularly significant expression of the radicalism of the Gospel is seen in the different 'evangelical counsels' which Jesus proposes in the Sermon on the Mount (cf. Mt 5-7), and among them the intimately related counsels of obedience, chastity and poverty. The priest is called to live these counsels in accordance with those ways and, more specifically, those goals and that basic meaning which derive from and express his own priestly identity" (*Pastores Dabo Vobis*, no. 27).

- Persistent accompaniment on the part of the bishop and of priest and lay friends, who together may support this priestly witness with respect, friendship, advice, and prayer

- Constant vigilance and prudent caution in his relationships with other persons

- A permanent capacity to work unsparingly so that Christ may be known, loved, and followed

- A life in community with other priests. St. Augustine maintained that it was advisable for celibate priests to live together in the same residence.

✠ The priest must use these means and methods in a constant and complementary way, in order to live his celibacy with serenity and joy.

In the light of what has just been presented, it will not be difficult to agree with what Pope Benedict XVI writes in the post-synodal apostolic exhortation *Sacramentum Caritatis* on the Eucharist as source and summit of the life and mission of the Church: "In continuity with the great ecclesial tradition, with the Second Vatican Council and with my predecessors in the papacy, I reaffirm the beauty and the importance of a priestly life lived in celibacy as a sign expressing total and exclusive devotion to Christ, to the Church and to the Kingdom of God, and I therefore confirm that it remains obligatory in the Latin tradition. Priestly celibacy lived with maturity, joy and dedication is an immense blessing for the Church and for society itself" (no. 24).

✠

For more on this topic, see the following pontifical documents:

Vatican Council II, *Presbyterorum Ordinis*; *Lumen Gentium*
Code of Canon Law
Pope Paul VI, *Sacerdotalis Caelibatus*, 1967
Pope John Paul II, *Pastores Dabo Vobis*, no. 27, 1992
Catechism of the Catholic Church, nos. 922, 1579, 1599, 1618-1620

XI
How to Pray

What is Christian prayer?

✠ Christian prayer is

- The elevation of the soul to God
- A gift of God and an action of the person
- A conversation, a relationship of the children of God with their Father, by means of the Son Jesus, in the Holy Spirit: a living relationship of covenant, of a communion of love
- A participation of the whole person, whatever the language (gestures and words) and the place of prayer
- A humble and trusting adherence to the will of God the Father
- A vital necessity. The Christian, for his or her spiritual life, has an absolute and incessant need for prayer, just as for air and water for biological life.

✠ Prayer flows from the Holy Spirit: "God sent the spirit of his Son into our hearts, crying out, 'Abba, Father!'" (Gal

4:6). It is the Spirit himself who prays in the Christian and teaches him or her "how to pray as we ought" (Rom 8:26).

✠ A humble and repentant heart, rich in faith, is required of the person who prays, who acknowledges himself or herself as created the image of God, redeemed by Christ, sanctified by the Holy Spirit: "Everything is possible to one who has faith" (Mk 9:23).

✠ God is the first to call each person incessantly to the mysterious encounter of prayer.

✠ Prayer therefore has a twofold dimension:

- Descending: an invitation to encounter and dialogue that the Father, through Christ, in the Holy Spirit, addresses to the person
- Ascending: a response of the person to the Father, through Christ, in the Holy Spirit

How did Jesus behave with regard to prayer?

✠ During his earthly life, he prayed

- According to the rhythms and the prayers of his people
- Frequently, including at night, in solitude, and in particular before the decisive moments of his mission
- Saying "Abba, Father." His is a filial prayer; it arises from the fact that he is the eternal Son of God.
- For us as our priest; in us as our Head and guide. He is prayed to by us as our God.

✠ The whole life of Jesus was an incessant prayer, profound and intimate communion with God his Father. His words and actions are the visible manifestation of this constant prayer.

✠ Jesus is the "teacher of prayer" for the Christian. Simply by praying, he teaches us how to pray. And at the same time, he gives precise indications on prayer. For example:

- "When you pray, say: Father" (Lk 11:2).
- "In praying, do not babble like the pagans, who think that they will be heard because of their many words . . . Your Father knows what you need before you ask him" (Mt 6:7-8).
- "When you pray, go to your inner room, close the door, and pray to your Father in secret" (Mt 6:6).
- "If you bring your gift to the altar, and there recall that your brother has anything against you, leave your gift there at the altar, go first and be reconciled with your brother, and then come and offer your gift" (Mt 5:23-24).
- "Pray for those who persecute you, that you may be children of your heavenly Father" (Mt 5:44-45).
- "Ask and you will receive; seek and you will find; knock and the door will be opened to you" (Lk 11:9). "Ask and you will receive, so that your joy may be complete" (Jn 16:24).
- "You do not possess because you do not ask. You ask but do not receive, because you ask wrongly" (Jas 4:2-3).

- "Seek first the kingdom (of God)" (Mt 6:33), and the heavenly Father will give the one who prays everything that he or she needs.

✠ To the question "Lord, teach us to pray" (Lk 11:1), Jesus responds by teaching the prayer of the Our Father. This prayer

- Is the synthesis of the entire Gospel
- Puts us in communion with the Father and with Jesus Christ. At the same time, it reveals us to ourselves.
- Contains seven appeals to God the Father. The subject of the first three is the glory of the Father: the sanctification of his name, the coming of the Kingdom, and the fulfillment of the divine will. The other four present him with our desires, they concern what our lives need to be fed, to be healed from sin, to be liberated from evil.
- With the final Amen, we express our fiat to the seven appeals: may it be thus.

What are the sources from which the Christian draws for prayer?

✠ They are

- The Word of God, contained in Sacred Scripture
- The liturgy of the Church, in particular the sacraments and the Liturgy of the Hours
- The theological virtues: faith, hope, and charity
- The present moment, with its everyday events, happy and sad

✠ It is good for the Christian to use all of these sources in a complementary way, always giving first place to the Eucharistic celebration, the source and summit of the whole life of the Christian and of the Church, as well as the model for all prayer.

Why is it important to use the Psalms as prayer?

It is important because the Psalms

- Are words of God addressed to the human person, and words of the human person addressed to God
- Are a prayer of the People of God: Christ associates the Church his spouse with himself. They are a public prayer, in which the Church is particularly involved.
- Contain the infinite spectrum of questions, situations in which people of every place and age can find themselves
- Are an expression of the varied sentiments of the human heart: joy, gratitude, thanksgiving, love, tenderness, enthusiasm, but also intense suffering, recrimination, request for help, and justice, which sometimes result in anger and imprecation. In the Psalms, the human being finds himself or herself whole and entire.
- Provide a living experience of the closeness of God in the everyday moments of existence that gave rise to the Psalms and of which they are the reflection
- Offer various intentions of prayer: to glorify God, to thank him, to express trust, to ask for help, to ask for forgiveness, to make one's prayer heard

- Offer expressions for "ejaculatory prayer," from the Latin word *iaculum*, or dart. These are very short expressions from the Psalms that can be recited throughout the day as brief but effective conversations with God and can also be "thrown," like flaming darts, for example, against temptations.

What are the main forms of Christian prayer?

☩ The main forms of prayer:

- In content:
  - The prayer of adoration
  - The prayer of request, which is centered above all on forgiveness, on the search for the Kingdom of God ("your kingdom come"), and also on every true necessity for ourselves and for others
  - The prayer of thanksgiving: "In all circumstances give thanks" (1 Thes 5:18). One gives thanks to God for the gifts of creation and redemption. Every event and every need can become a reason for thanksgiving.
  - The prayer of praise: one renders glory to God because he *is*, before and more than what he *does*.
- In the way of praying:
  - Vocal prayer: This, based on the unity of body and spirit in human nature, associates the body (in particular the voice) with the inner prayer of the heart. It is conducive to prayer with others.

- Meditative prayer: This brings into action thought, imagination, emotion, and desire. It can be assisted by a book (in particular the Bible), by icons, by writings of the Fathers of the Church and the saints, by the great Book of Creation, by everyday events . . .
- Contemplative prayer: This is a gaze of faith that is fixed upon Jesus, a silent love, "an intimate relationship of friendship, in which we often linger alone with the God who loves us" (St. Teresa of Jesus).

✠ Prayer "must on the one hand be something very personal, an encounter between my intimate self and God, the living God. On the other hand it must be constantly guided and enlightened by the great prayers of the Church and of the saints, by liturgical prayer . . . Praying must always involve this intermingling of public and personal prayer" (Pope Benedict XVI, *Spe Salvi*, no. 34).

✠ All of these forms of prayer are necessary and complementary in the life of the believer and of the Church.

✠ The Eucharist contains, expresses, realizes, and completes in a supreme manner all of these forms of prayer. There is no prayer that equals or surpasses the Eucharistic celebration.

How is the prayer of the Christian united with that of Christ?

This is what St. Augustine says in this regard: "When we address our prayer to God, we must not separate the Son from him, and when the Body of the Son is praying, this must not be considered as detached from the Head. In this way the same person, the one Savior of the Body, our Lord Jesus Christ, Son of God, will be the one who prays for us, prays in us, is prayed to by us. He prays for us as our priest, he prays in us as our Head, he is prayed to by us as our God . . . This is why we pray to him, through him, and in him; we speak with him and he speaks with us" (St. Augustine, *Commentary on the Psalms*: Psalm 85, 1).

What relationship is there between the prayer of the Christian and the Church?

Every authentic prayer of the Christian is also a prayer of the Church and in the Church. The Christian, in fact, is a member of the Church by virtue of Baptism. Therefore the Church, both the heavenly one and the one that is a pilgrim on the earth, prays with, in, and for the Christian. And the Christian prays in the Church, with the Church, and for the Church.

What is the connection between prayer and everyday life?

✠ Prayer requires consistency of life: observing the Word of God, his commandments, doing his will.

✠ One prays as one lives, and one lives as one prays.

✠ It is faith-filled, humble, trusting love that allows one to unite prayer with the whole of Christian life.

✠ In order that life may become a constant prayer, it is necessary that

- It be a life consistent with the teachings of the faith
- There be explicit moments during the day and week dedicated exclusively to prayer

When should one pray?

✠ "Pray without ceasing" (1 Thes 5:17).

- "Giving thanks always and for everything in the name of our Lord Jesus Christ to God the Father" (Eph 5:20)
- "With all prayer and supplication, pray at every opportunity in the Spirit" (Eph 6:18).
- "Pray without ceasing to the One who unites prayer with works and works with prayer" (Origen).

✠ It is always possible to pray: "It is possible even at the market or while walking alone, to make frequent and fervent prayer. It is possible even in your shop, both while you are buying and while you are selling, or even while you are cooking" (St. John Chrysostom).

What techniques are there for praying well?

✠ The history of Christian prayer has many techniques. Their purpose is to prepare the spirit and body for prayer, to support them during prayer, helping the person to recollection and concentration.

✠ These concern the words, the singing, the gestures, the iconography, and the place where one prays.

✠ Methods and techniques are necessary and helpful, but they are not automatically effective.

✠ These are means to assist prayer, but these cannot become ends.

✠ A method is nothing but a guide. The important thing is to advance, with the Holy Spirit, along the one Way, Model, Teacher of prayer: Jesus Christ.

What are the main objections to prayer?

✠ Here are some objections to prayer:

- I don't have time. I have more important things to think about and do.
- I don't want to; I don't feel like it.
- It is useless to pray, because what is really needed is action.
- I am unable to pray because I frequently get distracted, because my heart is dry, incapable of praying.

✠ These objections and difficulties can be overcome

- By exploring the meaning and value of authentic Christian prayer
- By praying and asking for God's help
- By taking into account that prayer certainly presupposes an effort and a fight against ourselves, against the snares of the Devil, against erroneous conceptions and various mindsets about prayer
- By growing in the virtues of humility, trust, perseverance, custody of the heart

✠ On the objection of those who say that they don't pray anymore because in the past they prayed a lot and were not heard, it is good to remember that God sometimes waits to listen to us or does not answer us at all in what we ask for

- In order to test our fidelity, constancy, trust in him
- In order to allow us to verify the authenticity, appropriateness, or necessity of what we are asking for, and especially the conformity of our requests with the will of God the Father
- In order to strengthen our faith
- In order to purify and improve our way of asking. St. James says, in fact: "You ask but do not receive, because you ask wrongly" (Jas 4:3).
- In order to avoid giving us something that is not our highest good. God knows us and loves us better than we know and love ourselves.
- Because he has something better and more useful to give us later. In fact, he sees better, further ahead, and deeper than we do.

✠

For more on this topic, see the following pontifical documents:

Catechism of the Catholic Church, Part Four

Compendium of the CCC, Part Four

Congregation for the Doctrine of the Faith: *Letter to the Bishops of the Catholic Church on Some Aspects of Christian Meditation*, 1989; Instruction on Prayers for Healing, 2000

XII
How Christians Meditate

What is Christian meditation?

✠ It is

- A silent, reverent listening to and obedient welcoming of the Word of God, in view of conforming all of one's life to it
- Being with God: "Remain in me, as I remain in you. Just as a branch cannot bear fruit on its own unless it remains on the vine, so neither can you unless you remain in me" (Jn 15:4).
- Approaching the mystery of union with God, which the Greek Fathers called the divinization of man: "God became man so that man might become God" (St. Athanasius).

- "Directed to the attainment of virtue and the love of God, and not to the acquisition of knowledge in general or of a particular psychological disposition" (St. Francis de Sales, *Introduction to the Devout Life*, Filotea, II, V)
- "A means of reflecting some of truth of the faith, in order to believe it with greater conviction, to love it as an attractive and concrete value, to practice it with the help of the Holy Spirit. It is a matter of a loving knowledge. It implies reflection, love, and practical intention. Its value lies not in thinking much, but in loving much" (CEI, *Catechismo degli adulti: La verità vi farà liberi*, no. 996).
- Indeed a focusing upon oneself, but also a transcending of one's ego, which is not God, but only a creature. God is *"interior intimo meo, et superior summo meo*: deeper in me than my own depths, and higher in me than my own height" (*Confessions*, 3, 6, 11). In fact, God is in us and with us, but he transcends us in his mystery.

✠ Christian meditation does not mean that the personal ego and its identity as creature should be annihilated and disappear in the ocean of the Absolute. In fact, "man is essentially a creature, and remains such for eternity, so that an absorbing of the human self into the divine self is never possible, not even in the highest states of grace" (*Letter to the Catholic Bishops on Some Aspects of Christian Meditation* [CM], no. 14).

What is the basis of Christian meditation?

It is based on

- The very reality of the One and Triune God, who "is love" (1 Jn 4:8), who has made us "adopted children," wherefore we can cry out with the Son in the Holy Spirit, "Abba, Father"
- Pondering the work of salvation that the God of the Old and New Testament has accomplished in history, through which God "speaks to men as friends and lives among them, so that He may invite and take them into fellowship with Himself" (*Dei Verbum*, no. 2)
- The Person of Christ the Lord, "in whom are hidden all the treasures of wisdom and knowledge" (Col 2:3). We must always have our gaze fixed on Jesus Christ, in whom divine love has been manifested and given to us above all on the Cross. "Thanks to the words, deeds, Passion and Resurrection of Jesus Christ, in the New Testament the Faith acknowledges in Him the definitive self-revelation of God, the Incarnate Word who reveals the most intimate depth of his love" (CM, no. 5). Christian meditation therefore requires constant growth in the knowledge of Christ, in such a way as to "comprehend with all the holy ones what is the breadth and length and height and depth, and to know the love of Christ that surpasses knowledge, so that you may be filled with all the fullness of God" (Eph 3:18-19).

- The constant willingness to do the will of God, on the example of Christ, whose "food is to do the will of the one who sent [him] and to finish his work" (Jn 4:34)
- The close correlation between the *lex orandi* and the *lex credendi*, between the manner of praying and the content of the Christian faith that is professed. Christian prayer is always determined by the structure of the Christian faith, in which the very truth of God and of the creature shines. "Prayer is faith in action: prayer without faith becomes blind, faith without prayer comes apart" (Cardinal Joseph Ratzinger, Conference for the presentation of the CM).
- Humility. The more a creature is permitted to approach God, the more reverence grows within it for God, the Thrice-Holy. It is that one understands the word of her who was gratified by the greatest possible intimacy with God, Mary Most Holy: "He has looked upon his handmaid's lowliness" (Lk 1:48), and also that of St. Augustine: "You can call me friend, I acknowledge that I am a servant" (St. Augustine, *Enarrationes in Psalmos* CXLU). "We can never, in any way, seek to place ourselves on the same level as the object of our contemplation, the free love of God; not even when, through the mercy of God the Father and the Holy Spirit sent into our hearts, we receive in Christ the gracious gift of a sensible reflection of that divine love and we feel drawn by the truth and beauty and goodness of the Lord" (CM, no. 31).

- Silence. We need to rediscover the value of silence, which creates a favorable atmosphere for reflection, contemplation, complete listening (to ourselves, to God, to others), the purification and unification of the person.
- Love of neighbor. Authentic meditation makes constant reference to love of neighbor, to action and passion, and precisely in this way draws closer to God. It stirs up an ardent charity in those who pray, driving them to work for the mission of the Church and the service of their brothers and sisters, for the greater glory of God.

What dimensions of the person are involved in meditation?

Meditation mobilizes all of the faculties of the human being: intelligence, memory, desire, will, attention, intuition, imagination, sentiment, the heart, behavior.

"This mobilization of faculties is necessary in order to deepen our convictions of faith, prompt the conversion of our heart, and strengthen our will to follow Christ. Christian prayer tries above all to meditate on the mysteries of Christ, as in *lectio divina* or the rosary. This form of prayerful reflection is of great value, but Christian prayer should go further: to the knowledge of the love of the Lord Jesus, to union with him" (CCC, no. 2708).

What is the importance of the body in Christian meditation?

✠ Human experience demonstrates that the position and attitude of the body are not without influence on the recollection and dispositions of the spirit, also involving the fundamental vital functions, like respiration and heartbeat. And this is because of the unity of the person, who is uni-dual: body and soul. In prayer, it is the whole person who must enter into relationship with God, and so the body must also take on the position most suitable for recollection.

✠ The importance of the body varies according to culture and personal sensibility.

✠ In any case, it is necessary

- To recognize the relative value of these physical stances. They are helpful only if they are used for the purpose of Christian prayer.
- To pay attention to the fact that these physical stances can degenerate into a cult of the body and can lead to the erroneous identification of all its sensations with spiritual experiences. "Some physical exercises automatically produce a feeling of quiet and relaxation, pleasing sensations, perhaps even phenomena of light and of warmth, which resemble spiritual well-being. To take such feelings for the authentic consolations of the Holy Spirit would be a totally erroneous way of conceiving the spiritual life. Giving them a symbolic significance typical of the mystical experience, when

the moral condition of the person concerned does not correspond to such an experience, would represent a kind of mental schizophrenia which could also lead to psychic disturbance and, at times, to moral deviations" (CM, no. 28).

What importance does technique have in Christian meditation?

✠ Christian meditation is not primarily a question of technique. It is in the first place and always a gift from God, of which the beneficiary feels unworthy. This gift can be granted only in Christ through the Holy Spirit.

The love of God is a reality that cannot be appropriated by any method or technique.

✠ Technique can offer an aid to Christian meditation.

What aids should be used to meditate well?

One can meditate reciting the Our Father calmly, slowly repeating a biblical phrase, looking with devotion at a sacred image. "We are usually helped by books, and Christians do not want for them: the Sacred Scriptures, particularly the Gospels, holy icons, liturgical texts of the day or season, writings of the spiritual fathers, works of spirituality, the great book of creation, and that of history—the page on which the 'today' of God is written.

"To meditate on what we read helps us to make it our own by confronting it with ourselves. Here, another book is opened: the book of life. We pass from thoughts to reality. To the extent that we are humble and faithful, we discover in meditation the movements that stir the heart and we are able to discern them. It is a question of acting truthfully in order to come into the light: 'Lord, what do you want me to do?'" (CCC, nos. 2705-2706). In this way, one proceeds along the path of holiness, in the life of perfection.

Are there stages in the life of perfection?

Christian tradition has distinguished three stages in the life of perfection:

1. *The way of purification*, which involves recognizing that one is a sinner and asking God's forgiveness for one's sins.
2. *The way of illumination*, which introduces the faithful, initiated into the divine mysteries, to knowledge of Christ through the faith that works by means of charity. It is made possible by the love that the Father gives to us in the Son and by the anointing that we receive from him in the Holy Spirit on the occasion of Baptism and Confirmation.
3. *The way of union with God*, realized through participation in the sacraments and the constant effort to live a moral life consistent with the Christian faith.

"With the passing of time, the exercise of meditation is simplified, and the heart prevails over reflection. We gradually arrive at the prayer of recollection. We are freed from particular images and thoughts, from memories, preoccupations, and projects. We turn a simple loving attention to God, to Jesus

Christ, to one of his perfections, to some salvific event. We remain in an attitude of loving silence before the Lord, who is present within us. We allow ourselves to be transformed by his Spirit, who can bring consolation or desolation, but never fails to purify us and strengthen us in charity. When the fervor of this experience tapers off, it is a good idea to return to discursive meditation or to vocal prayer" (CEI, no. 997).

What are the methods of meditation?

There are as many methods of meditation as there are spiritual teachers. But a method is nothing but a means, a guide; the important thing is to advance, together with the Holy Spirit, along the one way of prayer: Christ Jesus.

"From the rich variety of Christian prayer as proposed by the Church, each member of the faithful should seek and find his own way, his own form of prayer. But all of these personal ways, in the end, flow into the way to the Father, which is how Jesus Christ has described himself. In the search for his own way, each person will, therefore, let himself be led not so much by his personal tastes as by the Holy Spirit, who guides him, through Christ, to the Father" (CM, no. 29).

✠ Among the various methods, one is indicated by the Church as particularly good for meditating on Sacred Scripture: it is the one called *lectio divina*, which is a prayerful and meditative reading of the Word of God.

How is *lectio divina* done?

The spiritual Fathers usually indicate five steps in meditating on the Bible and describe them as follows:

- *Lectio.* In this first stage, I take the Bible not as just any sort of book, but like a treasure chest that contains the Word by which God speaks to me. I listen to a living word, which delivers a personal message to me. I listen to it as if it were for the first time. I make an effort to grasp its meaning in the most complete way possible. I encounter the light of God: it inhabits my intelligence and illuminates it.
- *Meditatio.* I invoke the Holy Spirit, that he may help me with the blindness of my mind. In humbly asking for light and in adherence to the faith, I pore over the Word with new attention. I discover how the ideas of God are different from those of human beings, and I realize how necessary it is to allow the Word of God to transform my convictions in order to conform them more and more to the ideas of God. I agree to change my mentality and my will in order to adhere to the mentality and will of God.
- *Oratio.* I make an effort to speak to God with all my heart, asking him to help me in my weakness. It is my moment to ask the Virgin Mary to communicate to me her prayer, made of trust and love, the fruit of her purity of heart. In her faith, in her adoring silence, in her innocence and courage to love and to receive the love of Jesus, I too dare to invoke her Son and ask him to help me. I learn from him to pray to

the Father in their Spirit of love. My heart learns to speak to God if it allows itself to be flooded with the love of Christ.

- *Contemplatio.* If I have allowed the Word, read and meditated upon, to illuminate the eyes of my heart and of my mind, if I have allowed myself to be fully penetrated by the meaning of Sacred Scripture to the point of developing a desire for constant intimacy with God, if I have prayed with boundless trust for my brothers and sisters and for the whole Church, then God responds. He infuses into my heart a certain inability to continue reflecting on his Word in a discursive manner, and he grants me a sort of participation in the fire of loving communion beyond all things that burns without beginning and without end within the Holy Trinity.
- *Actio.* In order to give me the gift of intimate and constant conversation with him, the Lord expects on my part that I increase at every opportunity my desire for and communion with his love.

What are the limitations of methods?

✠ The legitimate search for new methods of meditation must always take into account that

- Method cannot be detached from concept and understood as neutral with respect to what it conveys and to the cultural context in which it emerges

- It is necessary to respect the intimate nature of Christian prayer, which
  - Is "a personal, intimate and profound dialogue between man and God. It expresses therefore the communion of redeemed creatures with the intimate life of the Persons of the Trinity" (CM, no. 3; see also the section "How to Pray").
  - Can never be reduced to a method that could be used to free oneself from pain or even to obtain physical well-being, but is an openness to the love of God, to that love which did not hesitate before death, and death on the Cross
  - In order to be authentic, requires the encounter of two forms of freedom, the infinite freedom of God and finite human freedom
  - Is always realized in union with Christ, in the Holy Spirit, together with all the saints for the good of the Church

✠ With the limitations and risks of these methods taken into account, the Christian must listen with docility to and welcome with humility what the Church instructs, particularly through the popes and bishops: it is their responsibility, in fact, to "test all things and hold fast to that which is good" (*Lumen Gentium*, no. 12).

What are the mystical graces?

They are special graces, conferred by God for example "on the founders of ecclesial institutes to benefit their foundation, and on other saints, too, which characterize their personal experience of prayer and which cannot, as such, be the object of imitation and aspiration for other members of the faithful, even those who belong to the same institutes and those who seek an ever more perfect way of prayer" (CM, no. 24).

"It is not personal effort, but the action of the Holy Spirit that ushers us into mystical contemplation, and experience of God without concepts, without images, and without words. We can neither attain it nor prolong it as we wish; we can only prepare ourselves to receive it" (CEI, no. 998).

How long does Christian meditation last?

Habitual union with God, which is called constant prayer, is not necessarily interrupted when we also dedicate ourselves, according to the will of God, to work and to the care of our neighbor. "So whether you eat or drink, or whatever you do, do everything for the glory of God," the apostle Paul tells us (1 Cor 10:31).

St. Augustine says in this regard: "We know that the hermits of Egypt make frequent prayers, but they are all extremely brief. They are like rapid messages sent out to God. In this way the tension of the spirit, which is so necessary for the one who prays, remains always alert and fervent, and is not lulled to sleep by the excessive duration of prayer . . . So prayer should always steer clear of wordiness, but it should not overlook insistent supplication if fervor and attention are constant. The use of many words in prayer is equivalent to handling a necessary matter with superfluous words. Praying consists in knocking at God's door and invoking him with insistent and devoted ardor of the heart. The duty of prayer is better fulfilled with groaning than with words, with tears than with speeches" (St. Augustine).

Can the Christian also learn about meditation from other religions?

Can meditation practices (like Zen, yoga, controlled breathing, the mantra . . .) that come from the Christian East and from the great non-Christian religions constitute a suitable means for helping the person who prays to become fully open to God?

"Just as 'the Catholic Church rejects nothing of what is true and holy in these religions,' neither should these ways be rejected out of hand simply because they are not Christian. On the contrary, one can take from them what is useful so long as the Christian conception of prayer, its logic and requirements are never obscured. It is within the context of all of this that these bits and pieces should be taken up and expressed anew. Among these one might mention first of all that of the humble acceptance of a master who is an expert in the life of prayer, and of the counsels he gives. Christian experience has known of this practice from earliest times, from the epoch of the desert Fathers. Such a master, being an expert in '*sentire cum Ecclesia*,' must not only direct and warn of certain dangers; as a 'spiritual father,' he has to also lead his pupil in a dynamic way, heart to heart, into the life of prayer, which is the gift of the Holy Spirit" (CM, no 16).

✠

For more on this topic:

> Congregation for the Doctrine of the Faith, *Letter to the Bishops of the Catholic Church on Some Aspects of Christian Meditation*, 1989
>
> *Catechism of the Catholic Church*, Part Four
>
> *Compendium of the CCC*, Part Four
>
> Italian Episcopal Conference, *Catechismo degli adulti: La verità vi farà liberi* (CEI).

XIII
Lent

What is Lent?

✠ It is a special period of the liturgical year in which the Christian people prepares to celebrate the mystery of Easter.

✠ Lent is a favorable time to stand together with Mary Most Holy and St. John, the beloved disciple, beside Christ, who consummates upon the Cross the sacrifice of his life for all humanity (see Jn 19:25).

✠ "They will look upon the one whom they have pierced." It is the propitious time for gazing with trust at the pierced side of Jesus, from which flow "blood and water" (Jn 19:34)!

✠ "May Lent be for every Christian a renewed experience of God's love given to us in Christ, a love that each day we, in turn, must 're-give' to our neighbor, especially to the one who suffers most and is in need. Only in this way will we be able to participate fully in the joy of Easter" (Pope Benedict XVI, Message for Lent 2007).

Why forty days?

✠ The theology and spirituality of Lent developed in reference to events of the Old and New Testament.

✠ The number forty recalls

- The days of the universal flood
- The days spent by Israel in the desert
- The days spent by Moses on Sinai
- The days spent by the prophet Elijah in the desert before going to encounter God on Mount Horeb
- The days of penance of the inhabitants of Nineveh
- The days that Jesus spent fasting in the desert, at the end of which he was tempted by the Devil

✠ All of this has a didactic value. Lent is the time of

- The destruction of evil, as for the people of the flood
- Testing and of grace, as for Israel
- The prayer that disposes people for the encounter with God, as for Moses and Elijah
- Penance and expiation in view of the divine judgment, in imitation of the forty days of fasting and penance with which the inhabitants of Nineveh placated the divine wrath
- Fasting, undertaken for the purpose of eating the true bread, which is doing the will of the Father. "Not by bread alone does one live, but by every word that comes from the mouth of God" (as Jesus answered Satan at the end of the forty days spent in the desert).

What are the major themes of Lent?

There are three themes in particular that are presented to us by the Lenten liturgy:

1. *The theme of Easter*. Because Lent is a preparation for the Easter celebrations, the theme of death/life takes on primary importance. It begins on the second Sunday (the Transfiguration) and becomes more explicit during the last two weeks.
2. *The theme of Baptism*. In its fundamental structure, Lent is formed around the Sacrament of Baptism administered to adults during the Easter Vigil. Christians become more aware of their own Baptism.
3. *The theme of penance*. This is developed above all at the beginning of Lent (Ash Wednesday and the Gospel of the temptation of Jesus on the first Sunday). During Lent the Church, bride of the Christ who suffers and dies, lives the penitential aspect more intensely.

What are the Lenten practices?

✠ Lent involves an ascetical effort, individual and collective, the traditional forms of which are

- Prayer (daily Mass above all, and the Stations of the Cross)
- Fasting (all of the practices of mortification: of food, speech, entertainment, etc.). Mortification allows us to be more available for our neighbor, with more time for volunteer work and more money for charity.

- Almsgiving (help for our neighbor who is needier than we are)

✠ During Lent, the Church reminds us of the requirements of

- Fasting and abstinence from meat on Ash Wednesday and Good Friday
- Abstinence from meat every Friday of Lent

✠ The Church recommends in particular the practice, during Lent, of the corporal and spiritual works of mercy:

- The seven corporal works of mercy:

1. Feed the hungry.
2. Give drink to the thirsty.
3. Clothe the naked.
4. Give shelter to pilgrims.
5. Visit the sick.
6. Visit the imprisoned.
7. Bury the dead.

- The seven spiritual works of mercy:

1. Counsel the doubtful.
2. Instruct the ignorant.
3. Admonish sinners.
4. Console the afflicted.
5. Forgive offenses.
6. Bear wrongs patiently.
7. Pray to God for the living and the dead.

✠ These practices "express conversion in relation to oneself, to God, and to others" (CCC, no. 1434).

What is the importance of fasting?

(Cited from Pope Benedict XVI, Message for Lent, 2009)

✠ Today, Benedict XVI notes, fasting "seems to have lost something of its spiritual meaning," because it is often reduced to a "therapeutic value for the care of one's body."

✠ For the believer, however, fasting is of substantial importance, and is rich with numerous meanings and purposes.

- Personal dimension:

    "The believer, through fasting, intends to submit himself humbly to God, trusting in his goodness and mercy."

    The practice of fasting contributes to "conferring unity to the whole person, body and soul, helping to avoid sin and grow in intimacy with the Lord."

    "Denying material food, which nourishes our body, nurtures an interior disposition to listen to Christ and be fed by his saving word."

    In fasting and prayer, "we allow him to come and satisfy the deepest hunger that we experience in the depths of our being: the hunger and thirst for God."

    This practice is "a spiritual weapon to do battle against every possible disordered attachment to ourselves."

In the same way, it "helps the disciple of Christ to control the appetites of nature, weakened by original sin, whose negative effects impact the entire human person."

- Social dimension:

    The Holy Father also emphasizes the social significance of fasting, affirming that it "is an aid to open our eyes to the situation in which so many of our brothers and sisters live." When we save money by fasting, we can use it for beneficial, charitable works.

    This is why the pope urges parishes "to intensify in Lent the custom of private and communal fasts, joined to the reading of the Word of God, prayer and almsgiving."

✠ Fasting from food recalls and involves in particular fasting from sin (above all of gluttony, of the disordered use of sexuality, etc.).

✠ Ultimately, thanks to fasting, Lent is the ideal time "to cast aside all that distracts the spirit and grow in whatever nourishes the soul, moving it to love of God and neighbor."

On almsgiving:

✠ How should almsgiving be done? Here are some guidelines:

- It should be hidden. "Do not let your left hand know what your right is doing," Jesus says, "so that your almsgiving may be secret" (Mt 6:3-4).

- It should be done
  - Without offending others
  - Without putting ourselves on display (vainglory)
  - With joy. There is more joy in giving than in receiving (see Acts 20:35).
- Silence is best, far from the bright lights of media coverage.
- We should not limit ourselves to giving something material (money, bread . . .), but should give ourselves: our esteem, respect, our time, our talents (volunteer work).
- We should offer the material gift as a sign of the greatest gift that we can offer to others: the proclamation and witness of Christ.
- What gives value to almsgiving is love: see the passage about the widow's mite in the Gospel (Mk 12:42-44).

✠ What are the purposes of almsgiving?

- To help those who are in greater need
- To share with others what we possess thanks to God's kindness
- To practice the virtue of justice, even more than the virtue of charity
- To recognize Christ himself in the poor
- To imitate Christ, who became poor so that we might become rich
- To provide an ascetical exercise for us
  - To free us from attachment to earthly goods
  - To purify us within

- To affirm the principle that we are not owners, but rather administrators of the goods that we possess, given to us by God
- To act for the glory of God
- To practice it not out of philanthropy but out of charity and love: an act of ecclesial communion
- To bring us closer to God and to others: an instrument of authentic conversion and reconciliation with him and with our brothers and sisters
- To obtain the forgiveness of sins. St. Peter cites the forgiveness of sins as one of the spiritual fruits of almsgiving. "Love," he writes, "covers a multitude of sins" (1 Pt 4:8).

XIV
Mary

Who is Mary Most Holy?

Mary Most Holy

- Is a daughter of Israel, a young Jewish woman of Nazareth in Galilee, "a virgin betrothed to a man named Joseph, of the house of David" (Lk 1:26-27)
- "Stands out among the poor and humble of the Lord, who confidently await and receive salvation from Him. With her, the exalted Daughter of Sion, and after a long expectation of the promise, the times were at length fulfilled and the new dispensation established" (*Lumen Gentium*, no. 55).
- "Virgin Mother, daughter of your Son, more humble and more lofty than any other creature, the established end of eternal counsel, you are the one human nature so ennobled that its creator did not disdain to become its work" (Dante Alighieri, *Paradiso*, Canto XXXIII).

What relationship is there between Mary and Christ?

Jesus Christ was conceived in the womb of the Virgin Mary.

How did this conception take place?

By the work of the Holy Spirit, without the collaboration of man. "Mary was invited to conceive him in whom the 'whole fullness of deity' would dwell 'bodily.' The divine response to her question, 'How can this be, since I know not man?' was given by the power of the Spirit: 'The Holy Spirit will come upon you.' The mission of the Holy Spirit is always conjoined and ordered to that of the Son. The Holy Spirit, 'the Lord, the giver of Life,' is sent to sanctify the womb of the Virgin Mary and divinely fecundate it, causing her to conceive the eternal Son of the Father in a humanity drawn from her own" (CCC, nos. 484-485).

The virginal conception indicates that Jesus is truly Son of God. At the same time, it is a sign that salvation comes from God, from his superabundant grace, and not from us.

What does "Immaculate Conception" mean?

"God freely chose Mary from all eternity to be the Mother of his Son. In order to carry out her mission she herself was *conceived immaculate*. This means that, thanks to the grace of God and in anticipation of the merits of Jesus Christ, Mary was preserved from original sin from the first instant of her conception" (*Compendium of the* CCC, no. 96).

Mary, in that she was preserved from Original Sin, was therefore

- Redeemed
- Redeemed in a unique way, in a more eminent way
- Redeemed in advance
- Redeemed in anticipation of the Blood of Christ

In what sense is she all-holy?

✠ In the sense that she was never touched by any sin during her entire existence. She is "free from all stain of sin, fashioned by the Holy Spirit into a kind of new substance and new creature" (*Lumen Gentium*, no. 56). She is the "favored one" (Lk 1:28).

Is Mary ever-Virgin?

✠ The Christian faith affirms the real and perpetual virginity of Mary even in giving birth to her only Son Jesus, Son of God made man. She "remained Virgin in conceiving her Son, Virgin in birth, Virgin with child, Virgin mother, perpetual Virgin" (St. Augustine).

✠ Mary is Virgin in body and Virgin in soul: Mary, throughout her entire life, always entrusted herself completely to the will of God, she was always "the handmaid of the Lord" (Lk 1:38). "Mary is happier in receiving the faith of Christ than in conceiving the flesh of Christ" (St. Augustine, *De Sancte Virginitate*, 3, 3).

✠ The virginity of Mary also indicates the absolute and gratuitous initiative of God in her regard.

✠ After the birth of Jesus, Mary had no other children, remaining ever-Virgin before, during, and after birth.

Why does Sacred Scripture speak of brothers and sisters of Jesus?

✠ It was customary in the Old Testament and also among Jesus' contemporaries to call close relatives brothers and sisters as well.

✠ Jesus took it upon himself to say, stretching out his hand to his disciples: "Here are my mother and my brothers. For whoever does the will of my heavenly Father is my brother, and sister, and mother" (Mk 12:49-50).

✠ It must also not be forgotten that even in our day, priests call the lay faithful "brothers and sisters" to indicate the special bond that unites all in Christ Jesus.

What was Mary's connection with Jesus?

✠ Mary, throughout her whole earthly life, always preserved a special relationship with her Son Jesus. The earthly life of the Mother of God was characterized, in fact, by her perfect harmony with the person of the Son and by her total dedication to the work of redemption that he accomplished. "Embracing God's saving will with a full heart and impeded by no sin, she devoted herself totally as a handmaid of the Lord to the person and work of her Son. In subordination to Him and along with Him, by the grace of almighty God she served the mystery of redemption" (*Lumen Gentium*, no. 56).

✠ "This union of the Mother with the Son in the work of salvation was manifested from the time of Christ's virginal conception up to His death" (*Lumen Gentium*, no. 57).

✠ She was a faithful disciple of Christ. The response of Christ itself—Who is my mother? The one who does the will of my Father (see Mk 3:33-35)—which seems a bit offensive toward his Mother, in reality expresses the greatest possible praise of Mary, indicating that her true greatness lies precisely in the fact that Mary, before and above any other creature, did the will of God the Father.

What are the Mariological dogmas?

✠ They are

- The divine maternity of Mary (the title "Mother of God," or "Theotokos," was given at the Council of Ephesus in 431)
- Her Immaculate Conception (Pius IX, *Ineffabilis Deus*, December 8, 1854)
- Her perpetual virginity (Lateran Council, 649)
- Her Assumption into heaven (Pius XII, *Munificentissimus Deus*, November 1, 1950)

✠ These dogmas, although they were proclaimed at various points in the Church's history, are contained in divine Revelation and confirm the faith that has always been believed since the origin of the Church. They serve to define this faith in a more precise, solemn, and definitive way. "The Church's Magisterium exercises the authority it holds from Christ to the fullest extent when it defines dogmas, that is, when it proposes, in a form obliging the Christian people to an irrevocable adherence of faith, truths contained in divine Revelation or also when it proposes, in a definitive way, truths having a necessary connection with these" (CCC, no. 88).

✠ "There is an organic connection between our spiritual life and the dogmas. Dogmas are lights along the path of faith; they illuminate it and make it secure. Conversely, if our life is upright, our intellect and heart will be open to welcome the light shed by the dogmas of faith" (CCC, no. 89).

In what sense is Mary called the Mother of God?

✠ The Church proclaims Mary the Mother of God in that Jesus, who is truly her Son according to the flesh, is the Son generated by the eternal Father in the divine nature, the second Person of the Most Holy Trinity: himself God. Jesus Christ is "by nature Son of the Father according to the divinity, by nature Son of the Mother according to the humanity, but genuinely Son of God in his two natures" (Council of Friuli, Symbol, 796).

✠ "Mother of God," Theotokos, is the title officially attributed to Mary in the fifth century, more precisely at the Council of Ephesus in 431, but affirmed in the devotion of the Christian people as early as the third century. From the title "Mother of God" stem all the other titles with which the Church honors the Virgin Mary, but this is fundamental.

✠ After the Council of Ephesus, there was a true explosion of Marian devotion, and numerous churches were built and dedicated to the Mother of God. The Basilica of St. Mary Major in Rome is preeminent among these. The doctrine concerning Mary, Mother of God, found further confirmation at the Council of Chalcedon (451), at which Christ was declared "true God and true man . . . born for us and for our salvation of Mary, Virgin and Mother of God, in his humanity." As is well known, Vatican Council II assembled in the eighth chapter of the dogmatic constitution on the Church, *Lumen Gentium*, the doctrine on Mary, reiterating her divine maternity. The title of the chapter is "The Role of the Blessed Virgin Mary, Mother of God, in the Mystery of Christ and the Church."

What is the significance of the Assumption of Mary into heaven?

✠ Her Assumption into heaven, body and soul, signifies

- Complete conformity to her Son, who conquered death
- A special participation of Mary in the Resurrection of her Son
- A singular anticipation and prefiguring of our resurrection, which will take place at the end of time. It manifests to us the meaning and destiny of the body sanctified by grace.

✠ In the glorious body of Mary, material creation itself begins to take on some aspect of the risen Body of Christ.

What is the relationship between Mary and the Trinity?

There is a special relationship between Mary and the Most Holy Trinity, in regard to which she is Daughter-Bride-Mother: Daughter of God the Father, Bride of the Holy Spirit, Mother of the Son of God made man.

What is the relationship between Mary and God the Father?

✠ The marvelous works accomplished in Mary are the fruit of the primary and gratuitous action of God the Father. Mary responds to the free gift of God's grace and salvation with her prompt and total adherence of faith.

"Blessed are you who believed that what was spoken to you by the Lord would be fulfilled" (Lk 1:45).

✠ "From the beginning, Mary has constituted the great sign, with her maternal and merciful face, of the nearness of the Father and of Christ, together with whom she invites us to enter into communion" (Puebla Document, no. 282).

✠ By choosing her as Mother of all humanity, the heavenly Father intended to reveal, in a manner of speaking, the maternal dimension of his divine tenderness and concern for the people of every age.

What is the relationship between Mary and the Holy Spirit?

✠ The mystery of the Virgin Mary emphasizes the action of the Holy Spirit, who brought about the conception of the child within her womb and continually guided her life. The titles of Consoler, Advocate, and Auxiliatrix, attributed to Mary by the devotion of the Christian people, do not obscure, but rather exalt the action of the Consoler Spirit and dispose believers to benefit from his gifts.

✠ Mary's cooperation with the Holy Spirit, manifested in the Annunciation and in the Visitation, is expressed in an attitude of constant docility to the inspirations of the Paraclete.

✠ As a true woman of prayer, the Virgin asked the Holy Spirit to complete the work begun at the conception, so that the child might grow in "wisdom and age and favor before God and man" (Lk 2:52). Under this aspect, Mary is shown as a model for parents, demonstrating the need to go to the Holy Spirit to find the right way in the difficult task of child raising.

✠ Without a doubt, she was present at the pouring out of the Spirit on the day of Pentecost. The Spirit, who was already living in Mary, having worked wonders of grace in her, now descends again into her heart, communicating gifts and charisms necessary for the exercise of her spiritual maternity.

✠ Mary participates in the life and prayer of the first Christian community. St. Luke points out that the original community of the Church is composed not only of apostles and disciples, but also of women, among whom Luke names only "Mary the mother of Jesus" (Acts 1:14).

✠ Even now in the life of the Church, "she is called by the same Spirit to co-operate in a maternal way with him.

He continually revives the Church's memory of Jesus' words to the beloved disciple: 'Behold, your mother!,' and invites believers to love Mary as Christ loved her. As the bond with Mary grows deeper, so the action of the Spirit in the life of the Church becomes more fruitful" (Pope John Paul II, General audience, December 9, 1998).

What is the relationship between Mary and the Church?

Mary Most Holy is

- A member of the Church
- Mother of the Church
- Model of the Church
- Intercessor for the Church

In what way is Mary a member of the Church?

✠ She is our sister, a preeminent and entirely singular member of the Church.

✠ She is the first person to be redeemed, ransomed by Christ "in the most sublime manner" in her Immaculate Conception (see bull "Ineffabilis Deus" in Pio IX, Acta I, 605) and entirely renewed by and filled with the grace of the Holy Spirit.

Why is Mary the Mother of the Church?

- Since Mary is the Mother of Christ, she is also the Mother of the mystical Body of Christ, which is the Church. Paul VI was correct, therefore, during

Vatican Council II, on November 21, 1964, to attribute solemnly to Mary the title of "Mother of the Church." Precisely because she is Mother of the Church, the Virgin is also mother of each one of us, who are members of the mystical Body of Christ.

- She gave birth to a Son, whom God has made "the firstborn among many brethren (see Rom 8:29), namely, the faithful. In their birth and development she cooperates with a maternal love" (*Lumen Gentium*, no. 63).
- "Cooperating in the work of human salvation through faith and obedience" (*Lumen Gentium*, no. 56), she gave her assent in the name of all humanity.
- On Calvary, with the words, "Woman, behold, your son . . . Behold, your mother" (Jn 19:26-27), Jesus was already giving Mary in advance as Mother to all those who would receive the good news of salvation, and thus laid the foundation for their filial affection for her.
- Mary cooperates in the birth and development of divine life in the members of Christ, who we are. She is Mother of the Church in the order of grace.

✠ "The maternal duty of Mary toward men in no wise obscures or diminishes this unique mediation of Christ, but rather shows its power. For all the saving influences of the Blessed Virgin on men originate, not from some inner necessity, but from the divine pleasure. They flow forth from the superabundance of the merits of Christ, rest on His mediation, depend entirely on it, and draw all their power from it" (*Lumen Gentium*, no. 60).

In what sense is Mary the model of the Church?

✠ She is the figure and the most perfect realization of the Church. She is the model of the Church in maternity and in virginity.

- In maternity: "The Church . . . becomes herself a mother by accepting God's word in faith. For by her preaching and by baptism she brings forth to a new and immortal life children who are conceived of the Holy Spirit and born of God" (*Lumen Gentium*, no. 64).
- In virginity:
  - The Church "is a virgin, who keeps whole and pure the fidelity she has pledged to her Spouse. Imitating the Mother of her Lord, and by the power of the Holy Spirit, she preserves with virginal purity an integral faith, a firm hope, and a sincere charity" (*Lumen Gentium*, no. 64).
  - Without a doubt she constitutes for all the highest example of purity and total self-donation to the Lord. But in a special way she is the inspiration of Christian virgins and of those who dedicate themselves in a radical and exclusive way to the Lord in the various forms of consecrated life.
  - She encourages all Christians to make a special effort to live out chastity according to their particular state and to entrust themselves to the Lord in the diverse circumstances of existence. She who is the Shrine of the Holy Spirit par excellence helps believers to rediscover their

own bodies as temples of God (see 1 Cor 6:19) and to respect their nobility and holiness.

✠ "Hence the Church in her apostolic work also rightly looks to her who brought forth Christ, conceived by the Holy Spirit and born of the Virgin, so that through the Church Christ may be born and grow in the hearts of the faithful also. The Virgin Mary in her own life lived an example of that maternal love by which all should be fittingly animated who cooperate in the apostolic mission of the Church on behalf of the rebirth of men" (*Lumen Gentium*, no. 65).

✠ Mary is the eschatological image of the Church in the sense that she is already that which the Church, a pilgrim on the earth, will be one day at the end of this world. She, the one "full of grace," is already, in the eternity of heaven, the one "full of glory," of that glory in which humanity and the universe are called to share one day.

In what sense is Mary the model of the Church's holiness?

✠ Mary is all-holy, being "full of grace" (Lk 1:28). She represents for the community of believers the paradigm of authentic holiness, which is realized in union with Christ.

✠ "In the most holy Virgin the Church has already reached that perfection whereby she exists without spot or wrinkle (see Eph 5:27). Yet the followers of Christ still strive to increase in holiness by conquering sin" (*Lumen Gentium*, no. 65).

✠ On this journey toward holiness, believers in Christ feel encouraged by she who is the model of virtue.

✠ "Devotedly meditating on her and contemplating her in the light of the Word made man, the Church with reverence enters more intimately into the supreme mystery of the Incarnation and becomes ever increasingly like her Spouse" (*Lumen Gentium*, no. 65).

✠ Christian holiness is realized in an intense life of faith, hope, and charity. In all these three theological virtues, Mary is the exemplary model. In fact:

- *In faith*: Her example encourages the people of God to practice their faith and to explore and develop its content, keeping and meditating in their hearts upon the events of salvation.
- *In hope*: In listening to the message of the angel, the Virgin is the first to orient her hope toward the Kingdom without end that Jesus was sent to establish.
- *In charity*: Thanks precisely to the radiant charity of Mary, it is possible to preserve fraternal harmony and love within the Church in every age.

In what sense does Mary cooperate with the redemption?

✠ St. Augustine already attributes to the Virgin the description of Cooperator in the Redemption (see *De Sancta Virginitate*, 6; PL 40, 339), a title that emphasizes the joint and subordinate action of Mary with Christ the Redeemer.

✠ "In an utterly singular way she cooperated by her obedience, faith, hope, and burning charity in the Savior's work of restoring supernatural life to souls." Her universal maternity is the sublime fruit of this cooperation. "For this reason she is a mother to us in the order of grace" (*Lumen Gentium*, no. 61).

✠ The cooperation that the Lord God grants her is special. In union with Christ and in submission to him, she collaborated in obtaining the grace of salvation for all humanity in a unique and unrepeatable way, thanks to

- Her divine maternity in regard to Christ
- Her association with the sacrifice of Christ. In suffering with him as he died on the Cross, she cooperated in an entirely special way in the work of the Savior (see *Lumen Gentium*, no. 61).
- The particular contribution that she also makes to the life of the Church, of which she is Mother, down through the centuries and until the end of time, continuing to support the Christian community and all believers in their journey toward holiness and in their generous commitment to the proclamation of the Gospel

What is the relationship between Mary and women?

✠ "She is the one 'blessed among all women.' In her, God has conferred upon woman a dignity of unexpected dimensions. In Mary, the Gospel has permeated femininity, redeeming and exalting it. This is of capital importance for our cultural context, in which woman must be appreciated much more, while her place in society is being defined more clearly and broadly. Mary is the guarantee of feminine greatness, indicating the specific way of being woman, with her vocation of being soul, a donation capable of spiritualizing the flesh and incarnating the Spirit" (Puebla Document, no. 299).

✠ Mary fulfills in herself, in a sublime and paradigmatic way, the two dimensions or vocations of woman: virginity and maternity.

✠ Mary lived, in the specific and exclusive form of woman, the union between mother and child.

What kind of devotion is given to Mary?

✠ Since the beginning there has always been special devotion to the Virgin among Christians. Nonetheless, "after the Council of Ephesus the cult of the people of God toward Mary wonderfully increased in veneration and love, in invocation and imitation" (*Lumen Gentium*, no. 66). It is expressed in a special way in the liturgical feasts, among which, from the beginning of the fifth century, particular importance was taken on by "the day of Mary Theotokos," celebrated on August 15 in Jerusalem and adopted afterward as the Feast of the Dormition or Assumption.

✠ Marian devotion has developed up until our time in remarkable continuity, alternating flourishing periods with critical periods that nonetheless have often had the merit of promoting its renewal even more.

✠ "Mary was involved in the mysteries of Christ. As the most holy Mother of God she was, after her Son, exalted by divine grace above all angels and men. Hence the Church appropriately honors her with special reverence" (*Lumen Gentium*, no. 66).

This reverence is special in an unrepeatable way, because it is given to a person unique for her personal perfection and for her mission.

✠ "'This very special devotion . . . differs essentially from the adoration which is given to the incarnate Word and equally to the Father and the Holy Spirit, and greatly fosters this adoration.' The liturgical feasts dedicated to the Mother of God and Marian prayer, such as the rosary, an 'epitome of the whole Gospel,' express this devotion to the Virgin Mary" (CCC, no. 971).

✠ Therefore, the veneration of the faithful for Mary, although it is higher than the devotion shown for the other saints, is nonetheless lower than the worship of adoration reserved for God.

✠ However, there is continuity between Marian devotion and the worship given to God. In fact, the honor given to Mary is directed to and leads to the adoration of the Most Holy Trinity.

Christians' veneration of the Virgin promotes the worship rendered to the Incarnate Word, the Father, and the Holy Spirit. "The Church has endorsed many forms of piety toward the Mother of God, provided that they were within the limits of sound and orthodox doctrine. These forms have varied according to the circumstances of time and place and have reflected the diversity of native characteristics and temperament among the faithful. While honoring Christ's Mother, these devotions cause her Son to be rightly known, loved, and glorified, and all His commands observed" (*Lumen Gentium*, no. 66).

✠ To her, who has become Mother of the Church and Mother of humanity, the Christian people turn with childlike trust, to ask for her maternal intercession and obtain the benefits necessary for earthly life in view of eternal beatitude.

For more on this topic, see the following pontifical documents:

Vatican Council II, *Lumen Gentium*
Paul VI, *Marialis Cultus*, 1974
John Paul II, *Redemptoris Mater*, 1987
Catechism of the Catholic Church, nos. 484-511, 963-975
Compendium of the CCC, nos. 94-100, 196-199

XV
The Rosary

A. Historical Notes on the Rosary

When did praying the Rosary begin?

It has very ancient origins. In fact, it seems to go back to the twelfth century, when the Carthusians had already been reciting it for some time.

It quickly spread to the whole Catholic world, taking on different characteristics, but always preserving the invocation to Mary Most Holy. The popularity of the Rosary is also confirmed by the great number of confraternities and societies that, both in the past and in our own time, have named themselves after it.

The liturgical commemoration of Our Lady of the Rosary is celebrated on October 7.

It was Pope Gregory XIII who transferred it to this day, replacing the Feast of St. Mary of Victory, which his predecessor, St. Pius V, had instituted to commemorate the defeat of the Turkish fleet at the Battle of Lepanto.

What have some of the popes said about the Rosary?

After rapidly spreading through the Church, the Rosary was quickly regulated, officially recognized, and recommended to the faithful by the Supreme Pontiffs.

✠ The pope who first determined its essential structure, gave it its ecclesial charism, extolled its benefits, and recommended it to the People of God was the Dominican St. Pius V. Memorable are the bull *Consueverunt* of 1569, a true Magna Carta of the Rosary, and *Salvatoris Domini* of 1572, written after the victory of Christendom at Lepanto.

✠ Another great pontiff of the Rosary was Pope Leo XIII. Highly devoted to this prayer himself, he dedicated no fewer than twenty-two documents to it. He singled it out as "an easy way to infuse and inculcate the mind with the principal dogmas of the Christian faith."

In the year 1883, he established that "the whole month of October of the year underway and for the future be consecrated and dedicated to the heavenly Virgin of the Rosary." From the year 1891, we recall the significant definition that he made of the Rosary: "Like the calling card of our faith, it is the *Compendium* of the devotion due to Mary." In 1892, he justified his recommendations to pray the Rosary by saying that in it "are so well and so usefully united an excellent form of prayer, an efficacious means to preserve the faith, and an outstanding ideal of perfect virtue: it is absolutely correct that true Christians should have it in their hands often, and should meditate on it devoutly." In 1898 he went so far as to affirm that "the Rosary constitutes the most excellent form of private prayer and the most efficacious means to attain eternal life" and that "in the final hour the devotees of the Rosary will be consoled by the maternal tenderness of the Virgin Mary and will gently fall asleep in her bosom."

✠ Pope St. Pius X respected and loved the Rosary, praying it faithfully before and during his pontificate. He affirmed, "The Rosary constitutes the form of prayer par excellence, uniting with meditation on the mysteries of our religion and the most holy prayers the mediation of the Most Holy Virgin. We should nourish the dearest hope that by means of this practice, the Lord may grant us the greatest graces." In his will, he recommended the Rosary as "the prayer that, after the liturgy of course, is the most beautiful of all, the most rich in graces, the one most pleasing to the Most Holy Virgin Mary."

✠ The Rosary has been exalted and recommended in important encyclicals and speeches by Benedict XV and Pius XI, to whom is attributed the provocative phrase, often quoted: "I could convert the world if I had an army that recited the Rosary."

✠ For his part, Pius XII made the famous definition: "The Rosary is the synthesis of the entire Gospel, a meditation on the mysteries of the Lord, evening sacrifice, crown of roses, hymn of praise, prayer of the family, *Compendium* of Christian life, sure sign of heavenly favor, stronghold of the salvation to come."

✠ John Paul II, on October 16, 2002, published the apostolic letter *Rosarium Virginis Mariae* on the occasion of the 120th anniversary of the encyclical *Supremi Apostolatus Officio* with which Leo XIII, on September 1, 1883, inaugurated the publication of a series of documents dedicated precisely to the Rosary.

Although "clearly Marian in character," as John Paul II wrote in the introduction to the letter, the Rosary "is at heart a Christocentric prayer." "Simple yet profound, it still remains, at the dawn of this third millennium, a prayer of great significance, destined to bring forth a harvest of holiness." John Paul II proclaimed the year from October 2002 to October 2003 "The Year of the Rosary," calling all to the recitation of this prayer, which "goes to the very heart of Christian life; it offers a familiar yet fruitful spiritual and educational opportunity for personal contemplation, the formation of the People of God, and the new evangelization."

B. The Structure of the Rosary

How many Hail Marys are there in the Holy Rosary?

There are 200 Hail Marys, subdivided into decades, grouped into four cycles of five mysteries each. The Rosary is made up of five decades. The device of the rosary emerged as an instrument for counting prayers on the model of similar instruments already in use among other religions, in particular among the Buddhists (108 beads) and the Muslims (99 beads, the same as the number of names attributed to God by the Koran). Leo X, for example, approved in 1516 a "crown" in honor of our Lord that consisted of 33 small beads (for the years of Christ's earthly life, according to popular tradition) for the recitation of Our Fathers, with the addition of five larger beads (for the wounds of Christ) for the recitation of five Hail Marys.

Why was the Holy Rosary once made up of 150 Hail Marys?

The Holy Rosary of 150 Hail Marys recalled the 150 Psalms that are part of the Liturgy of the Hours and that, in the past (but also sometimes in the present), were replaced with the daily recitation of 150 Our Fathers for the illiterate. With the development of Marian devotion, the recitation of 150 Hail Marys was proposed to the people, when this biblical prayer did not yet have the second part, added toward the end of the fifteenth century.

What is the importance of the Hail Mary?

"The first part of the Hail Mary, also taken from the Gospel, lets us listen again each time to the words that God addressed to the Virgin through the Angel and to the words of her cousin Elizabeth's blessing. The second part of the Hail Mary resounds like the answer of children who, in addressing supplications to their Mother, do nothing other than express their own adherence to the saving plan revealed by God. Thus the thought of those who pray remains ever anchored to Scripture and to the mysteries presented in it" (Pope Benedict XVI, Meditation at Pompeii, October 19, 2008).

C. Importance of the Rosary

What is the relationship between the Rosary and daily life?

✠ "Our heart," John Paul II affirmed during the first year of his pontificate, "can enclose in these decades of the Rosary all the facts that make up the life of the individual, the family, the nation, the Church and mankind" (*Angelus*, October 29, 1978). And the pope dwelt precisely upon the "anthropological significance" of the Rosary, calling it "the 'secret' which leads easily to a profound and inward knowledge of Christ," but also a way to ask Christ for help with "all the problems, anxieties, labors and endeavors which go to make up our lives" (*Rosarium Virginis Mariae*, nos. 29, 24, 25). The Rosary is also a response to that "renewed demand for meditation" (no. 28) typical of our age.

✠ The Rosary is

- A precious spiritual means to grow in intimacy with Jesus, and to learn at the school of the Blessed Virgin always to fulfill the divine will
- School of contemplation and silence
- Simple and accessible to everyone
- Completely interwoven with scriptural elements (Meditation at Pompeii)

In what sense is the Rosary the prayer for peace and for the family?

Peace and family: these are, for Pope John Paul II, two particular areas in which the prayer of the Rosary shows itself capable of giving "reason to hope for a brighter future."

✠ "The Rosary is also a prayer for peace," John Paul II writes in *Rosarium Virginis Mariae*, "because of the fruits of charity which it produces," which include "the desire to welcome, defend and promote life, and to shoulder the burdens of suffering children all over the world"; to "bear witness to his 'Beatitudes' in daily life," to "act as a 'Simon of Cyrene' for our brothers and sisters weighed down by grief or crushed by despair." In a word, to become "peacemakers in the world" and to "hope that, even today, the difficult 'battle' for peace can be won."

✠ Another critical aspect of our time for which John Paul II requested special efforts is that of the family. The restoration of the Rosary in Christian families can constitute, according to the pope, an excellent opportunity to

- Nourish the family prayer that is so important even today
- Entrust the course of the children's maturation to the prayer of the Rosary
- Help parents to bridge the cultural gap between the generations
- Rediscover the value of silence
- Foster togetherness and communication in prayer among the various members of the family

Is the Rosary a Marian prayer?

The Rosary is not primarily a prayer addressed to Mary, but a prayer with Mary. It is therefore not a Marian prayer, but an essentially Christological prayer. The mysteries that it presents are centered on the main character: Christ Jesus. "It is first of all necessary to let the Blessed Virgin take one by the hand to contemplate the Face of Christ: a joyful, luminous, sorrowful and glorious Face. Those who, like Mary and with her, cherish and ponder the mysteries of Jesus assiduously, increasingly assimilate his sentiments and are conformed to him" (Meditation at Pompeii).

Is there also a missionary Rosary?

Yes, and it is very evocative: one decade, the white one, is for old Europe, that it may be capable of regaining the power of evangelization that generated so many Churches. The yellow decade is for Asia, which is exploding with life and youth. The green decade is for Africa, tried by suffering, but open to the proclamation. The red decade is for America, the cradle of new missionary energy. The blue decade is for the continent of Oceania and Australia, which is awaiting a more deeply rooted diffusion of the Gospel.

D. The Mysteries of the Rosary

✠ The joyful mysteries (Mondays and Saturdays):

- In the first joyful mystery, we contemplate the Annunciation of the angel to Mary Most Holy: "And coming to her, he said, 'Hail, favored one! The Lord is with you.' . . . Behold, you will conceive in your womb and bear a son, and you shall name him Jesus" (Lk 1:28, 31).
- In the second joyful mystery, we contemplate the visitation of Mary Most Holy to St. Elizabeth: "When Elizabeth heard Mary's greeting, the infant leaped in her womb" (Lk 1:41).
- In the third joyful mystery, we contemplate the birth of Jesus in the cave of Bethlehem: "[Mary] gave birth to her firstborn son. She wrapped him in swaddling clothes and laid him in a manger, because there was no room for them in the inn" (Lk 2:7).

- In the fourth joyful mystery, we contemplate the presentation of Jesus at the Temple by Mary and Joseph: forty days after the birth of Jesus, Mary and Joseph "took him up to Jerusalem to present him to the Lord" (Lk 2:22).
- In the fifth joyful mystery, we contemplate the finding of Jesus at the Temple: "'Did you not know that I must be in my Father's house?' . . . His mother kept all these things in her heart" (Lk 2:49-51).

✠ The luminous mysteries (Thursdays):

- In the first luminous mystery, we contemplate the Baptism of Jesus in the Jordan: "It happened in those days that Jesus came from Nazareth of Galilee and was baptized in the Jordan by John. On coming up out of the water he saw the heavens being torn open and the Spirit, like a dove, descending upon him. And a voice came from the heavens, 'You are my beloved Son; with you I am well pleased'" (Mk 1:9-11).
- In the second luminous mystery, we contemplate Jesus at the wedding of Cana: "His mother said to the servers, 'Do whatever he tells you.' . . . Jesus did this as the beginning of his signs in Cana in Galilee and so revealed his glory, and his disciples began to believe in him" (Jn 2:5, 11).
- In the third luminous mystery, we contemplate the proclamation of the Kingdom of God: "Jesus came to Galilee proclaiming the gospel of God: 'This is the

time of fulfillment. The kingdom of God is at hand. Repent, and believe in the gospel'" (Mk 1:14-15).

- In the fourth luminous mystery, we contemplate the Transfiguration of Jesus: "About eight days after he said this, he took Peter, John, and James and went up the mountain to pray. While he was praying his face changed in appearance and his clothing became dazzling white" (Lk 9:28-29).

- In the fifth luminous mystery, we contemplate the institution of the Eucharist: "While they were eating, Jesus took bread, said the blessing, broke it, and giving it to his disciples said, 'Take and eat; this is my body.' Then he took a cup, gave thanks, and gave it to them, saying, 'Drink from it, all of you, for this is my blood of the covenant, which will be shed on behalf of many for the forgiveness of sins'" (Mt 26:26-28).

✠ The sorrowful mysteries (Tuesdays and Fridays):

- In the first sorrowful mystery, we contemplate the agony of Jesus in Gethsemane: "He was in such agony and he prayed so fervently that his sweat became like drops of blood falling on the ground" (Lk 22:44).

- In the second sorrowful mystery, we contemplate the scourging of Jesus: "Then Pilate took Jesus and had him scourged" (Jn 19:1).

- In the third sorrowful mystery, we contemplate the crowning of Jesus with thorns: "Weaving a crown out of thorns, they placed it on his head" (Mt 27:29).

- In the fourth sorrowful mystery, we contemplate Jesus carrying his Cross to Calvary: "Then [Pilate] handed him over to them to be crucified. So they took Jesus, and carrying the cross himself he went out to what is called the Place of the Skull, in Hebrew, Golgotha" (Jn 19:16-17).
- In the fifth mystery, we contemplate the Crucifixion and Death of Jesus: "There they crucified him . . . When Jesus had taken the wine, he said, 'It is finished.' And bowing his head, he handed over the spirit" (Jn 19:18, 30).

✠ The glorious mysteries (Wednesdays and Sundays):

- In the first glorious mystery, we contemplate the Resurrection of Jesus: "I know that you are seeking Jesus the crucified. He is not here, for he has been raised just as he said" (Mt 28:5-6).
- In the second glorious mystery, we contemplate the Ascension of Jesus into heaven: "The Lord Jesus, after he spoke to them, was taken up into heaven and took his seat at the right hand of God" (Mk 16:19).
- In the third glorious mystery, we contemplate the descent of the Holy Spirit upon the Apostles and Mary Most Holy in the upper room: "Then there appeared to them tongues as of fire, which parted and came to rest on each one of them. And they were all filled with the holy Spirit" (Acts 2:3-4).
- In the fourth glorious mystery, we contemplate the Assumption of Mary Most Holy into heaven: "The

Mighty One has done great things for me, and holy is his name" (Lk 1:49).

- In the fifth glorious mystery, we contemplate the coronation of Mary Most Holy as Queen of Heaven and Earth: "A great sign appeared in the sky, a woman clothed with the sun, with the moon under her feet, and on her head a crown of twelve stars" (Rev 12:1).

For more on this topic, see the following pontifical documents:

Paul VI, *Marialis Cultus*, no. 46)
John Paul II, *Rosarium Virginis Mariae*

XVI
Indulgences

What are indulgences?

✠ "Indulgences are the remission before God of the temporal punishment due to sins whose guilt has already been forgiven. The faithful Christian who is duly disposed gains the indulgence under prescribed conditions for either himself or the departed. Indulgences are granted through the ministry of the Church which, as the dispenser of the grace of redemption, distributes the treasury of the merits of Christ and the Saints" (*Compendium of the* CCC, no. 312).

✠ "The gift of the indulgence manifests the fullness of God's mercy, which is expressed in the first place in the Sacrament of Penance and Reconciliation. This ancient practice, about which there has been no lack of historical misunderstandings, must be properly understood and received. Reconciliation with God, although it is a gift of God's mercy, implies a process to which the human person contributes through personal effort and the Church through its sacramental mission. The journey of reconciliation is centered on the Sacrament of Penance, but even after the forgiveness of sin obtained through this sacrament, the human being remains marked by those 'residues' which make him or her not entirely open to grace and in need of purification and of that total renewal of the person by virtue of the grace of Christ, which the gift of the indulgence is of great help in obtaining" (Apostolic Penitentiary, *Il dono dell'Indulgenza*).

✠ The practice of indulgences must therefore be understood as an expression and embodiment of the mercy of God, who helps his children to wipe out the punishment due for their sins, but also and above all to drive them on toward a greater fervor of charity.

How are indulgences connected to the Sacrament of Confession?

Indulgences are closely connected to the Sacrament of Confession in that they are the remission before God of the temporal punishment due to sin, already remitted in terms of guilt with the Sacrament of Confession.

What are the characteristic elements of the indulgence?

✠ The indulgence

- Is the remission of the temporal punishment due to sin
- Is obtained through the Church

- Can be
  - Partial
  - Total
- Can be applied to oneself or to the deceased

✠ Let's examine these elements by degrees and in greater detail.

1. The Indulgence Remits the Punishment

What are the punishments in question?

✠ Sin, whether mortal or venial, even when it is forgiven in terms of guilt through the Sacrament of Penance, leaves in the sinner "residues," "traces," "dark areas."

✠ These "residues," traces," "dark areas" are expressed in

- Bad habits
- Disordered affections and attachments to creatures
- The disposition to venial sin (egoism, pride, laziness . . .)
- Promptings, more or less strong, to fall back into sin
- Weakness of the will to oppose the tendency to sin
- A sort of inner apathy in prayer, in the love of God, and in works of charity

✠ These "residues" of sin deserve "temporal punishment," which the Christian must satisfy in this life or in Purgatory in order to be totally purified in such a way as to be admitted to the vision of God in heaven.

✠ The punishment is therefore the effect of sin, which entails both guilt (remitted with the Sacrament of Confession) and punishment.

✠ "It is a divinely revealed truth that sins bring punishments inflicted by God's sanctity and justice. These must be expiated either on this earth through the sorrows, miseries and calamities of this life and above all through death, or else in the life beyond through fire and torments or 'purifying' punishments" (Pope Paul VI, *Indulgentiarum Doctrina*, no. 2).

Of what kind can the punishment be?

It can be of two kinds:
1. *Eternal*, which
    - Entails eternal separation from God
    - Is a consequence of mortal sin
    - Is removed, together with the guilt, with confession
2. *Temporal* (the effect of venial sin)

What does the punishment indicate?

The reality of the punishment indicates

- The existence of sin:
  - Its gravity
  - The consequences/damage that it produces in us, in others, in creation . . .
- The need to repair this damage
- The chastisement that we deserve: chastisement/punishment understood as healthy medicine, which helps us to
  - Become aware of sin
  - Remedy its consequences
  - Free ourselves from it
- The infinite mercy of God, who, while condemning sin because he is just and holy, at the same time is infinitely merciful and patient with the sinner, forgiving the sin, remitting the punishment, giving his grace
- Life after death (the last things)
- The need for complete purification in order to enter into heaven
- Purgatory for the expiation of the remaining punishments
- The unity of exchange-assistance with the deceased. The indulgence requested by the living for their deceased assists the purification of those in Purgatory who are waiting to be admitted into heaven.

2. The Indulgence Is Obtained Through the Church

✠ Christ wants to associate the Church with himself, in accumulating and dispensing its spiritual riches obtained from him solely through his sacrifice of Death and Resurrection.

✠ This manifests and actualizes

- Above all the unity, solidarity, and interdependence in the Church: the communion of saints (see CCC, no. 1475), the exchange of spiritual goods, the bond of communion among Christians in
  - Converting
  - Making reparation
  - Publicly and privately condemning sin
  - Asking God for the mitigation and/or elimination of punishments
- The magisterial role of the Church: the Church minister/mother who, by the will of Christ, its Head, dispenses the benefits acquired from Christ himself to the advantage of its members and of all humanity

3. The Indulgence Can Be Plenary or Partial

✠ The indulgence is partial or plenary depending on whether it liberates in part or in full from the temporal punishment due to sin.

✠ Both partial and plenary indulgences can always be applied to the deceased by way of suffrage.

✠ A partial indulgence can be acquired more than once a day unless there is a specific indication to the contrary. A plenary indulgence, however, can be acquired only once a day.

✠ The plenary indulgence can be daily, annual, or occasional.

How does one obtain the daily plenary indulgence?

In various ways. By

- Adoring the Most Holy Sacrament for at least half an hour
- Devoutly reading Sacred Scripture for at least half an hour
- Devoutly praying the Stations of the Cross
- Reciting the Holy Rosary (at least one complete cycle of five decades) at church or as a family
- Visiting the cemetery. The believer who devoutly visits a cemetery from November 1-8 and prays, even

only mentally, for the deceased, is granted an indulgence applicable only to the deceased.

How does one obtain an annual or occasional indulgence?

The Church also offers various ways to receive a plenary indulgence throughout the year:

- Devout reception, even only over the radio, of the blessing imparted by the Supreme Pontiff to the world (*Urbi et Orbi*)
- Participation in spiritual exercises for at least three days
- A devout visit to the parish church on the feast of the patron or on the August 2, the day of the indulgence of the "Porziuncola" (the *Perdono d'Assisi*)
- The renewal of baptismal promises at the Easter Vigil and on the anniversary of one's own Baptism
- Other particular circumstances indicated by the Holy See

What are the conditions for the acquisition of a plenary indulgence?

✠ The believer becomes disposed to receive a plenary indulgence by fulfilling these external and internal signs of participation:

1. Making an effort to develop an interior attitude of affective and effective detachment from all sin

2. Celebrating worthily (even twenty days before or after) the Sacrament of Penance, to open the heart to mercy. With a sacramental confession, one can acquire more than one plenary indulgence.
3. Participating devoutly in the Holy Eucharist (even in the days before or after)

✠ When the plenary indulgence requires a visit to a church, one must recite the Creed, the Our Father, and a prayer for the intentions of the Holy Father.

How are partial indulgences obtained?

There are many ways to obtain "partial" indulgences. They are ordinarily combined with the recitation of a certain prayer or ejaculation, and/or with the performance of acts of charity and penance, for example: pilgrimages, prayers, charitable works for the poor, public witness to the faith, renunciations, voluntary asceticism, abstinence from unnecessary consumption (smoking, alcoholic beverages, etc.), fasting, abstinence from meat (or from other foods according to the specifications of the bishops' conference), giving a suitable sum to the poor, acceptance of sufferings, prayers and works of suffrage for the deceased . . . All of this helps to express conversion of heart.

✠

For more on this topic, here are some pontifical documents:

Paul VI, *Indulgentiarum Doctrina*, January 1, 1967

Apostolic Penitentiary, *Enchiridium Indulgentiarum*, quarto editur (July 16, 1999); *The Gift of the Indulgence*, January 29, 2000

Catechism of the Catholic Church, 1471-1479